Memories
OF
Mark

Memories OF *Mark*

My Life
with Mark Prophet

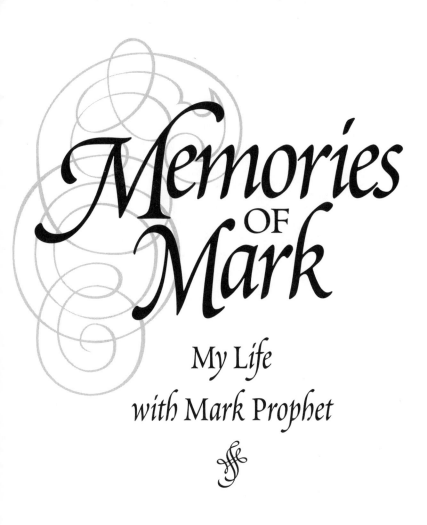

ANNICE BOOTH

SUMMIT UNIVERSITY PRESS®

MEMORIES OF MARK
My Life with Mark Prophet
by Annice Booth
Copyright © 1999 by Summit University Press.
All rights reserved.

Library of Congress Card Catalog Number: 99-63576
ISBN: 0-922729-50-6

SUMMIT UNIVERSITY 🕭 PRESS®
Summit University Press and 🕭 are registered trademarks.

Printed in the United States of America.

04 03 02 01 00 99   6 5 4 3 2 1

CONTENTS

PREFACE

IN A TIME WHEN SO MANY are searching for a guru,* for a teacher, for a mentor, for meaning to life, I was fortunate to have found all of these through The Summit Lighthouse. There are many paths, many teachers, many gurus who set themselves up in the midst of followers who earnestly seek the light. And then, there was Mark Prophet!

Mark was a master psychologist. He could read the heart and soul of any man or woman. He was simple and yet profound. He was a messenger* of God, sponsored by the Great White Brotherhood* to set forth the teachings of the ascended masters for the age of Aquarius. He could inspire you to believe in yourself by saying, "You can make it if you TRY! What man has done, man can do!"

Mark lived in the twentieth century. He faced the same temptations and trials of everyday life that we experience today. He knew exactly what are the pitfalls of daily existence, for he did not have an easy life, by any means.

And yet he conquered. He became a wayshower and an example for all of us. He is holding out his hand, now that he is ascended, to help us over the rough places and to find our way home.

If we can only accept the love that he is offering us, we too can be victorious as he was, and rise above the depression and darkness and despair into which so many have fallen. *There is meaning to life!* And that can be glimpsed by holding fast to the hand of the ascended masters and accepting their teachings and their love.

Mark L. Prophet and his twin flame,* Elizabeth, founded The Summit Lighthouse,* a worldwide spiritual organization that is helping thousands to find their way out of human problems and into the sunlight of a new day of hope and happiness.

*We have placed words which may be unfamiliar in a glossary at the back of the book.

They were interested in every phase of life—founding a Montessori school for children up to grade twelve. The Prophets truly believed in the potential of the child, including their own four children. These students were taught not only to read and write but also to have a sense of self-esteem and self-worth and to accept themselves as children of God.

Mark opened the Four Winds Organic Center in Colorado Springs. This was a restaurant, health food store and juice bar dedicated to full and vibrant health for all seekers. Young people who were traveling around the country, "hippies" as they were called in the '60s, searching for a meaning to life and for a guru who could teach them, were drawn to the Four Winds.

And after they once met Mark Prophet, many stayed and joined the staff of The Summit Lighthouse. They had found what they had been seeking. Mark was able to communicate his love to all who came to his door, and these young people found a warm family waiting for them.

Mark's plans for a self-sufficient community were brought to fruition by Elizabeth Clare Prophet after his ascension.* The Royal Teton Ranch was established in Montana near Yellowstone National Park. Organic gardening, emphasis on physical and mental health and healing, nutritious food, exercise and hiking in the beautiful Rocky Mountains of the retreat were all a part of Mark's plan for the new-age man and woman.

Mark was a physical man living in our everyday world and yet, at the same time, he was so close to God that he was truly an adept. He possessed yogic powers as much as any guru you could find in the Himalayas (although he seldom displayed them).

Words cannot describe how my life has been made richer by this contact with Mark Prophet. My gratitude can only be expressed by trying, to the best of my ability, to follow his example and bring the knowledge of his teachings and those of the ascended masters to the world. I know that there are thousands who are hungry for these truths, just as I was. I also know that these teachings can transform lives.

I have included anecdotes from my life on the staff of The Summit Lighthouse with Mark L. Prophet from 1966 until 1973, when he made his transition and ascended back to the heart of God from whence he came.

Please don't let the fact that I may have given a rather conversational and humorous slant to this tale distract you from the seriousness, the truth and the beauty of the teachings of the ascended masters. Mark was definitely fun to be with, but on the instant his consciousness could soar to untrammeled heights—and take you with him to cosmic consciousness, if you were willing.

It seemed to me that, after Mark's ascension, wherever I would go I would always hear, "Annice, tell us a story about Mark." And so, for those who did not know him as I did, I have written my "stories about Mark" in this little book.

Will you follow with me through the pages of *Memories of Mark: My Life with Mark Prophet*? Let me introduce this prophet to you.

CHAPTER ONE

A Tribute: Mark the Man, Mark the Adept

In an era when the world decries its lack of true leaders and heroic role models, one of the greatest was right in our midst—Mark L. Prophet. As is often the case, he was not recognized by the many for being the great soul, which, in reality, he was.

He said, "Ours must be a message of infinite love and we must demonstrate that love to the world." That was Mark Prophet.

"All of life is God. All of being is God. All of consciousness is God." Not only was this his philosophy but he also lived that love every day in his personal life. We see him as altogether human, as we all are, and yet all the while he fulfilled his divine potential.

I think the most important aspect of Mark's message to us is that love, God's love, is victorious. It is meant to be, and if we claim it, then it *will* be. And love is what this world needs most today.

Mark Prophet was one of the greatest examples of that love that I can ever hope to see. And I am grateful for the opportunity to have lived and worked with him for seven years in Colorado Springs at our world headquarters known as La Tourelle and in Santa Barbara at the Motherhouse. I was given an opportunity daily to see and benefit from his love in action.

Mark was indeed a holy man for the people. He did not hide away in a cave in the Himalayas and pray and meditate (although he did have the attainment to do so). He came forth into the midst of the people, sponsored by the Ascended

Masters El Morya and Saint Germain.* He loved to mingle and chat with everyone he met.

There could be no question about the fact that Mark was a devotee, and yet he was firmly grounded on earth. El Morya once remarked that "your spirituality is expressed by your practicality." Mark was a very practical man who had a tender concern and loving care for every person on his staff and, in fact, for everyone he met.

I have often thought that Will Rogers' observation "I never met a man I didn't like" applied equally well to Mark Prophet. He would show his concern for others on an everyday practical level and yet be able to inspire them to seek a higher level of spiritual attainment.

Mark was a master psychologist. He could read the heart and soul of a man and always seemed able to give that person a very balanced, down-to-earth message that was just exactly what that soul needed at the moment.

I soon realized that no matter how much I loved and respected Mark as a person, I also saw that he was a great adept and that a part of him was always close to heaven. In later chapters I shall relate some examples of his contact with the ascended masters* and his own God Presence.

Mark Prophet was a messenger of God, sponsored by the Great White Brotherhood* to set forth the teachings of the ascended masters for the Aquarian age. He said that it was his assignment to found a movement that would encompass the entire world, or at least lay the foundation for that expansion so thoroughly in his lifetime that the mission could be fulfilled in the next few years by his twin flame, Elizabeth.

In a previous embodiment he was the author of the Gospel of Mark in the New Testament. And he was also sent in this age by the ascended masters to proclaim the climax of the two-thousand-year mission of Jesus Christ in the Piscean age. In addition, his assignment was to bring the message of Jesus' second coming in the hearts of lightbearers.

Mark L. Prophet

When I lived back at La Tourelle in Colorado Springs, the headquarters of The Summit Lighthouse that Mark founded, I don't think many of the staff recognized the great adept with whom we were living. Some saw him as a human man and criticized him for his human frailties and failings. I don't believe they realized the great powers and spiritual attainment Mark possessed until it was too late and he had ascended. It has always been a great sorrow to my heart to realize what some staff members missed.

Mark said that the masters had forbidden him to use

phenomena (i.e., supernatural powers) in this lifetime, and because of this some people were blind to the true significance and attainment of his lifestream and mission. El Morya said that the founders of the Theosophical Movement in the late nineteenth century had performed feats of phenomena in their attempts to make known to the world the reality of the inner planes. That experiment failed to produce the receptivity that the masters had desired. Many people were caught up in the glamour and outer manifestations that they saw and failed to see the true inner meaning of the teachings.

I have often thought that if Mark Prophet had been presented to the world as an Indian guru in a robe and turban, that many more would have been attracted to the movement. However, that was not the masters' plan for Mark's mission this time around.

Mark Prophet and his Guru, El Morya, were so closely identified that I could never separate the two of them and discern which of them was speaking at the moment. I soon stopped even trying. Morya lived in Mark's aura.

One of my earliest recollections of conversations with Mark that illustrate this point occurred when we had just returned from our trip to Europe in 1968. I was not even on the staff of The Summit Lighthouse at that time but had been granted a few glimpses of the adept that Mark really was on the European tour.

I remember that I said, "Mark, I have just finished reading in Saint Germain's early books from the I AM Activity* that any of us who sincerely apply ourselves can make our ascension either in this lifetime or the next." And I said, "But what puzzles me is, if we all need to have your attainment before we can ascend, how are any of us are going to make it?"

He answered, "Well, Mrs. Booth, I want you to know that 'all things are relative except the Absolute.'" While I was pondering that for a moment, he added, "Now, you remember that the master wants you to know that." I was in a state of total shock to realize that the Ascended Master El Morya had actually given me a message.

That sentence was an excellent summation of Mark's philosophy: God is your Absolute, and everything else is relative. One of the most important benefits of the teaching I received from Mark, as I think back over the many conversations I have had with him, were just these isolated instances of short sentences that remain in my consciousness even today.

Another little sentence that I shall always remember was spoken at a time in 1969 when we were repairing our new focus in Santa Barbara and preparing it for eventual use as the Ascended Masters' Motherhouse. (More about that later.) The building was in a sad state of disrepair and neglect, and the best and fastest way to prepare it for painting was a thorough sandblasting operation.

I had been serving back at La Tourelle, helping prepare the final manuscript of *Climb the Highest Mountain* for publication while a crew of four men remained in Santa Barbara to work on the reconstruction of the Motherhouse.

One time Mark, Elizabeth, a few staff members and I drove out to Santa Barbara to see how the repairs were progressing. I was absolutely horror-struck when I entered my house on the property for the first time in several months and found a two-inch-thick layer of sand dust covering the entire place, both inside and out.

When Mark saw my dismay, he said, "Mrs. Booth, this was necessary in order to have a truly beautiful ascended master focus. And the master wants you to know that 'a man cannot be perfection until he sees perfection.'" Apparently my sense of perfection at that moment was not as clear as Mark's and Morya's.

The name "Mark" means "Mother of the Ark," and, indeed, Mark did mother all life. He nurtured every soul he met in order that that soul might rise up and be one step higher on the Path. The Ascended Master Kuthumi* paid him a tribute in a *Pearl of Wisdom** dictated after his ascension: "They sing of Mark, whom they call the 'Mother of the Ark,' for he nourished the flame of the ark of the covenant and drew therefrom the eternal message of salvation to God's chosen people."

One of the things I remember most about Mark was his childlike humility and compassion. He was no respecter of persons—a humble man who truly loved life and yet he would not stand for anyone's human nonsense, no matter who they were. He was completely uninhibited, spontaneously speaking whatever was in his heart at the moment. You never knew what was going to happen next or what he was going to say.

We read: "Except ye be converted, and become as little children, ye shall not enter into the kingdom of heaven." (Matt. 18:3) Well, Mark Prophet was certainly one of Jesus' little children. He had this childlike quality of adoration, of absolute dedication to the will of God, of absolute obedience to the ascended masters. He was childlike but certainly not childish. There is a world of difference.

Mark was never afraid or ashamed to allow the Holy Spirit to express through him at any time or in any situation. It was often those of us who were with him who were embarrassed, not Mark. There are many anecdotes in his life that I would love to share with you about his unexpected actions, and

The Prophet family at Tatiana's first birthday party

perhaps I shall in succeeding chapters.

I've never experienced so much love in any one individual—love for both God and man. It just radiated out from him in every way—in his prayers and invocations, his sermons and talks, the dictations that the ascended masters delivered through him in poetry and song, in his cares and concerns for practical living, in business decisions and in just plain loving life and loving people, including, of course, his beloved twin flame, Elizabeth.

Along with the love he had for the masters, he also truly and deeply loved the so-called ordinary and common folk, or as the Bible says, "the meek and lowly." I think one of the reasons he loved jokes and anecdotes was that, like Jesus' parables, anyone could understand them. His sermons and lectures were replete with these. He was drawing from memories of his former lives as Aesop, the teller of fables, and the poet Longfellow.

Mark had the distinct ability to deflate the pomposity and overstuffiness of the outer self. He would never let you miss the great seriousness of life and its true initiations, but neither would he allow you to take yourself too seriously. For instance, at any moment he could suddenly burst out singing the theme song from the radio show of "Little Orphan Annie," including Sandy's dog bark at the end, or start wrestling with you, or suddenly leap up into the air, slap you on the back, pull a laughing bag out of a drawer, tell a joke or recite some nonsensical line of verse such as:

> The Chevy is my auto;
> I shall not want another.
> It leadeth me beside the repair shop.
> It vexeth my soul.
> I anoint its tires with patches.
> Its radiator runneth over.
> Its rods and pistons annoy me.
> It has a breakdown in the presence
>   of mine enemies.

> And if this thing shall follow me
>   all the days of my life,
>   I shall dwell in the bughouse forever.

For those of you who did not know Mark Prophet in person, as a contrast to the previous "nonsensical lines of verse," he also wrote beautiful prayers and decrees that were a sublime poetry evoking the presence of God.

Mark Prophet was a twentieth-century master, interpreting for us the Lord's mysteries while at the same time, remaining strongly tethered to this physical plane. He would teach us that we, as well as he, are both human and divine. As he wrote when he was Longfellow:

> Lives of great men all remind us
> We can make our lives sublime
> And, departing, leave behind us
> Footprints on the sands of time.
>   —*A Psalm of Life, Stanza 7*

Then one day, February 26, 1973, Mark took his leave of us. He told Elizabeth when he married her that he would not be here very long and that one day Saint Germain would transfer to her the mantle of messenger.

And so, after twelve years, he personally demonstrated what he had been teaching. He accelerated his consciousness into the light of the ascension. He lived in the modern-day world, as we do. He faced the same problems we face daily. He overcame his limitations and, by his great love, ascended back to the heart of God—victor over time and space.

Mark is a wonderful example to all of us and a wise counselor on the path of initiation. We are grateful for the depth of his communion with the Lord's hosts, for the love and wisdom of his heart and for the disciplines of life without which no one can be victorious on the Path, as he was.

He now stands with us as the Ascended Master Lanello, the Ever-Present Guru. He is saying to you and to me that we can make it in this very life—if we TRY!

CHAPTER TWO

MARK'S EARLY YEARS

Born in Chippewa Falls, Wisconsin

Mark told us that he had memories of other realms as a child. He remembered when his soul was drawing near for the final integration of consciousness with the body. It was on December 24, 1919, Christmas Eve, a cold winter night. He saw his father, with his overcoat fastened against the wind, crossing the bridge on his way home to his mother who was in labor. The next thing Mark remembered was his soul descending through the birth canal before the immediate moment of birth. He remembered the angels' songs as they were drawn around him. And then he remembered actually entering the birth canal saying, as Jesus did, "Lo, I am come to do thy will, O God." He told me that each of us makes this vow before coming into embodiment but, of course, we might not remember it as Mark did.

He was born in a little house in Chippewa Falls, Wisconsin. I actually saw that home while I was living in Minneapolis. Mark was born not only with a memory of inner realms but also with a consciousness of the past. He could communicate with the beings that peopled the heaven-world without needing the language of earth.

Let's let Mark tell us in his own words:

"I remember when, in the first year of my life, I was in my baby buggy with a mosquito netting over me, under a lilac bush. I went out of that body and floated up to a white cloud that was probably 5,000 or 8,000 feet above me. I was surrounded with bright and shining beings.

Mark at age 2

"There were angelic beings in the clouds. We had beautiful conversations there, admiring the earth below. They knew me and I knew them. After we concluded our conversations, I silently dropped down and came back to the lilac bush, went through the netting and woke up screaming for my bottle. I remember. I have never forgotten it."

As a small child Mark remembered his coming and going

in and out of his body many times, frolicking with the nature spirits and angelic beings and entering into very high states of consciousness. He remembered discoursing with the ascended masters and then returning back to his three- or four-year-old body, playing outside in the sandbox or along the stream in the backyard.

Let's let Mark continue his recollections:

"When I was a small boy, I used to leave the body and go down into the earth and travel in subterranean streams with the nature spirits of the water element known as undines.* I knew these undines as well as I know your faces, and I would swim in and under the water with the undines.

"When I entered school and began to study some of the fairy stories, I was amazed to find that there were parallels in some of these nature stories that recalled for me some of my out-of-the-body experiences.

"So, I was a bit of a different child than most people. I know why now, but I didn't then."

Mark was a very devotional child and yet he often got in trouble with the neighbors because he could see their auras and read their minds and did not yet have the discrimination not to tell people what he saw. He was not too popular with the adults because of his special gifts.

He said he could read minds as easily as most people can read a book. He often had his face slapped (literally) because he was telling some lady in his mother's Ladies Aid Society what she was thinking. He was too accurate. And so he learned the hard way not to tell people what he saw and heard.

His Father's Death

When Mark was only nine years old, his father died after a long illness. He deeply loved his father and felt the loss keenly. He related to us how before the funeral the coffin was on display in their living room. He was so overcome by grief that he put his hand on his father's body as a form of last farewell. This caused the wheels upon which the casket rested to move a few inches. For years afterwards, neighbors were talking about how "that terrible Prophet boy" was pushing his father's casket all over the room.

In those days there was neither Social Security nor any welfare, and so his mother had to earn a living. She did this by selling yards of cloth door–to–door. She had little squares of material for samples that she would show people and then take their orders. Mark said that when he was a little boy, she patched his pants with those squares, and they didn't match at all.

Can you imagine that little fellow being laughed at in school because his pants were patched with mismatched colors and patterns? Perhaps it was a lesson in humility and an opportunity for him to balance his past incarnations of wealth and authority.

His Prayer Closet in the Attic

Mark told us about his early life. He said that he was a very orthodox young man and that he searched throughout all the fundamentalist churches in town for what he knew within himself was Truth. He built a little prayer closet in the attic of his home in Chippewa Falls and spent hours at a time on his knees praying to Jesus—in the blistering heat of summer and the freezing cold of winter. He remembered the verse in the Bible "When thou prayest, enter into thy closet" (Matt. 6:6), and he took this literally.

He used to love to witness at prayer meetings and especially when evangelists would come to town. Apparently the light* that he bore antagonized many of those in the congregations and they did not want him to participate in their worship services. They didn't even want him in their churches. And yet Mark knew Jesus personally and tried to tell them what Jesus was teaching him. As a result, he spent more and more hours alone with Jesus, on his knees in his little prayer closet in the attic.

The Ascended Master El Morya

Meeting El Morya

Although Mark was very close to Jesus, he did not know any of the other masters of the Great White Brotherhood until one day when he met El Morya.* After his father's death, Mark had to go to work to help support his mother—in fact, he did not even quite finish high school.

He first received the call from the Master El Morya when he was still in his teens. Mark was working as a section hand on the Soo Line Railroad, laying steel.

It was a hot day and the sun was beating down. Mark heard the bell of a shunting engine coming toward him. As he was about to bring the pick down, he was suddenly surrounded by a cloud of light and in another plane. In a communication that seemed to last five minutes—but in reality was only an instant, the split second between when he raised the pick and brought it back down—the Master El Morya appeared to him. He told Mark that he had a mission and said that the masters would come to him every day to teach him some of the mysteries of life. El Morya also told him of an event soon to happen that would verify that what he was saying was true.

Mark thought he must have been hallucinating from the heat and from reading too many adventure stories. Then the next morning he heard a knock at the door, and the Western Union boy was there with a telegram—with the proof—just as El Morya had told him.

Since he was very devoted to his fundamentalist training, Mark was unable to reconcile this turbaned Eastern adept with his lifelong devotion to Jesus. After a few months he decided that Morya might not be an authentic representation of the Christ but, in fact, of the devil, since he had never heard these teachings in his church. And so he asked El Morya to leave. The master drew himself up to his full seven-foot height, bowed and said, "Very well, my son. As you wish, so shall it be," and withdrew.

It was only later, after many years, that Mark realized what he had lost and begged him to come back and be his teacher. El Morya finally returned. And when he did, he eventually sent Mark to Washington, D.C. to found The Summit Lighthouse.*

World War II

In the army during the Second World War, the same thing happened as when he was a youth in Chippewa Falls. Mark

Mark in air force uniform, World War II

always read his Bible and prayed. And that is not exactly what most soldiers do in army barracks. And so, as in Chippewa Falls, he was not very popular with the men in the service.

Mark had an inner attunement with the masters but, as a result, did not have an easy life as a young man.

CHAPTER THREE

FOUNDING THE SUMMIT LIGHTHOUSE

MARK had been working as an emissary of the Brotherhood prior to 1958, the year when he actually founded The Summit Lighthouse.

Madonna

The earliest mention we have of his activities is in December of 1950 when he wrote a book entitled *Madonna*. This story is a good example of Mark's openness to Eastern teachings. It shows his early ability to synchronize Eastern precepts with those of the Bible, with which he was so familiar. This work also contains some ideas that were quite progressive for his time. As far as we can tell, this manuscript was never published. However, he used the concepts in it as foundational material for groups that he started throughout the East and Midwest and for his lectures throughout the country.

The Order of the Holy Child

Mark continued his dream of universal brotherhood when he founded the Order of the Holy Child, in 1951. His goal was that the order of the holy child, begun so long ago by Saint Joseph and Mary and Jesus as the holy family, should continue until all mankind know that every child and every man and woman is holy unto God, as precious unto him as the day that he gave them birth.

This Order of the Holy Child was sponsored by Jesus, Kuthumi and Mother Mary for the protection of the child, and for the education of the child. It is a teaching of science, health and abundance. It is the teaching and training of the child of your heart and other children in the path of service, freedom and holy orders.

Mark formulated a pledge and a membership statement, which he sent to every member of the legislature in Washington, D.C. I would like to quote from this letter.

I am forming a sacred order composed of legislators and rulers, as well as citizens interested in embracing the embodied principles. This order is simply called, the "Order of the Holy Child."

There are no dues, no rules, except that you promise to devote one minute per day to reading a few words inscribed on the certificate of membership, which you will post on the wall of your office. There are no meetings except a meeting of mind and heart before God and the promise to stand face-to-face with this certificate and submit your conscience to the little child in any matter embodying a decision affecting the lives of others.

This will constitute membership in the Order of the Holy Child—a mere living the principles of this order that our civilization may evolve to a higher level. Catch the vision, the lovely, beautiful vision, of what this can mean to our civilization, ripe now for either fruition or destruction, rise or decline.

Send a copy to the governor of your state and to others. You have my permission to publicize this letter via the press and radio in the interest of the great destiny of America under God, mindful now as never before of our future, our posterity. Out of our acts of today grow all of our tomorrows. Let us publicize this idea abroad and give it life.

This is only an excerpt from his letter, but it shows clearly the heart of Mark Prophet. And then he told us of the great burden on his heart when the concept of the Order of the Holy Child was not accepted by either the legislators or the clergy. The movement never even got off to a start. In fact, he was sure that many of his letters were tossed in the wastebasket.

Just think for a minute. If this idea of the ascended masters had been accepted in 1951, what kind of a world would we be living in today? No abortion, no child abuse, no drug and alcohol problems because children would be truly accepted and loved. What other problems burdening our society today could have been forestalled if this movement had swept the nation?

However, Mark's love for the child bore fruit in another avenue. Today all of America is aware that our children have been betrayed by education. Many numbers of private schools have been formed. We started our own Montessori International School in Colorado Springs in 1970.

Mark Prophet came and, like many pioneers in his time, he laid the foundation but was largely unrecognized. However, the ideas that he carried are the ideas of the Christ and cannot forever be set aside.

He used to say, "Had the world accepted the teachings of the I AM Presence and the violet flame, had it been in every church and synagogue and mosque in this nation, had the schools accepted it, what a different place the world would be!"

The Order of the Holy Child was intended to be caught as a mighty torch passed from heaven through the runner, Mark L. Prophet.

Ashram Notes

In 1951 Mark was also touring around the country and starting Ashram groups.* These were meant to be little candles of light all over the land drawing down the light of God. And each person whom he contacted was supposed to start a little prayer group with seven members.

He sent monthly messages from the ascended masters to

each of these small groups—suggestions for meditation and prayer for world conditions. We have since collected these early writings and published them in a volume entitled *Ashram Notes* (see bibliography). El Morya's goal, which Mark carried out, was to found an ashram of world servers held together through prayer and meditation.

The Brotherhood of the Ark of the Covenant

Mark spent much of his time prior to the founding of The Summit Lighthouse in 1958 traveling throughout the East and Midwest, lecturing and holding seminars. He established a group called The Brotherhood of the Ark of the Covenant in January of 1954. Lectures were held monthly at the First Spiritual Science Church in Madison, Wisconsin.

For the next several years, Mark continued to send out *Ashram Notes* to a small group of devotees and also continued as a guest lecturer at various organizations.

Our timeline is a bit sketchy at this point, but he was also a member and lecturer of the Rosicrucian Order as well as a member of Paramahansa Yogananda's Self-Realization Fellowship. He gave lectures during this time for the Self-Realization Fellowship in Madison, Wisconsin.

Washington, D.C., 1958

In 1958, El Morya sent Mark Prophet to Washington, D.C. to lay the foundation for a worldwide movement to publish the teachings of the ascended masters. Mark said he did not know what to do, did not know how to do it, and had no money to fund the project. He said he told Morya, "Yes, of course, I'll go. But I don't have any staff and I don't have any money." Morya just answered, "Do it!"

Mark tells us that he started out with four people whom Morya had sent to help him, a small rented room on Kentucky Avenue in Washington, D.C., a typewriter, a bread board, two candles and a 300-watt lightbulb. He said that if he was supposed to found a Lighthouse of Light, he felt that he needed to have plenty of light. And so he bought this 300-watt lightbulb. Later he received as gifts an antique Chinese rug, a statue of Gautama Buddha and a large picture of El Morya.

Here is a description of those early days in Mark's own words: "I was desperately in search of a mission. It had taken every last cent to my name to get there [Washington, D.C.]. How would you like to be in the position I was in at that time? I was told by Morya to go to Washington to found The Summit Lighthouse, and I knew only one or two people in the entire city. And they knew a couple more people, and so my congregation was exactly four. We were in this one room with nothing to signify that this organization would ever get off the ground. There were just that 300-watt light bulb swinging from the ceiling, four chairs—and faith."

I am telling you this because I think many of us are tempted to take for granted the founding of The Summit Lighthouse. We often don't realize how difficult it was, how much obedience to the master it required for Mark to leave his home in the Midwest and go to Washington to found an organization about which he knew virtually nothing. He only knew that he loved the Ascended Master El Morya who told him that the Brotherhood needed him in Washington, D.C.

Mark remembered the assignment Morya had given him of founding a worldwide religion, but by now, he was beginning to wonder if what he was doing was right because there was no physical evidence of the birth of the movement—only the command of El Morya to go to Washington.

Morya's Answer to Mark

One day Mark was so discouraged that he did something he had never done before: he asked El Morya to give him a physical sign to bolster his faith. Mark said, "In all the years I have known you, Morya, I have never asked you to do anything. Now, will you please do something for me?" He was accustomed to talking to Morya's picture as to an old friend.

There was an old Sears Roebuck phonograph in the room and a very old record called "Hearts and Flowers" that he used for his meditations. He had played that record so many times that a deep groove had been worn in it. And when the needle came to that place, it just kept going round and round, rrr, rrr, rrr, until you lifted it by hand and placed it over to the right spot.

Mark looked at the large picture of El Morya in the sanctuary and said, "I believe, but please show me just one sign that you are real." Mark relates that a brilliant ray of light shot out from that picture and hit him in the heart like a bolt of lightning so strong that he staggered. His whole body had become charged with electricity.

He said, "Morya, will you please pick up this needle, which is now stuck in this groove?" Morya sent another ray of light, picked up the phonograph arm with this ray of light, slid it over about a quarter of an inch and gently set the needle down on the proper place on the record. Mark said that he felt the strong vibration of God, and a holy radiation permeated the room as the record continued to play. Now he knew for sure that Morya had answered him and that he was doing the right thing. And he never doubted him again, even in some of his darkest moments of testing and trial.

Choosing a Name

At one point Mark asked El Morya, "What are we going to call this organization?" At that moment a strong wind came in the window, knocked a volume of Longfellow's poems off the table, turned the pages one by one and stopped at the poem *The Lighthouse*. And so they decided upon the name "The Summit Lighthouse."

The Heart, Head and Hand Decrees

Mark said he was in his car in Washington, D.C. about 5:00 a.m. on a snowy, winter morning, driving his son around to deliver his newspapers. Suddenly, El Morya appeared and said, "I want to give you some decrees." Mark looked high and low in his car for some paper and finally tore up a paper bag he found on the back seat. He wrote down these decrees in about five minutes as Morya dictated them. And so these decrees have been with The Summit Lighthouse since the very beginning, known to us from that moment as the Heart, Head and Hand Decrees.

These Heart, Head and Hand Decrees* contain the matrix for our ascension. In them we are walking the steps of Jesus' own ascension. It takes but a few minutes to give these eight short decrees. In fact, El Morya has recommended that we give them daily, preferably in the morning before we start our day.

The Ascended Master Founding Fathers

When The Summit Lighthouse was first started under El Morya's direction, there were really two branches: The Summit Lighthouse headquarters in Washington, D.C. and the Lighthouse of Freedom in Philadelphia, under the direction of Frances Ekey, who had worked with the Ballards in the I AM Movement and subsequently with the Bridge to Freedom. She joined her group in Philadelphia with Mark's in Washington in the early days of The Summit Lighthouse under the direction of the Master El Morya.

August 7, 1958 was the day of the formal establishment of The Summit Lighthouse by the Ascended Master El Morya through the Messenger Mark L. Prophet. On that day Mark Prophet, Frances Ekey, and Christel Anderson gathered in Philadelphia for the first board meeting. Seven ascended masters—Archangel Michael,* Elohim of Peace,* Saint Germain, Maha Chohan, El Morya, Gautama Buddha and Godfre—delivered dictations releasing the original dispensation for The Summit Lighthouse.

Thirty-three years later, on August 11, 1991, these same

---

*We have included the words to these decrees in the glossary.

seven "founding fathers" returned again to dictate and deliver their dispensations on the thirty-third anniversary of The Summit Lighthouse.

Mark Prophet had ascended on February 26, 1973, and so the dictations were given this time through the messenger, Elizabeth Clare Prophet. In 1961, then a student at Boston University, she had responded to the call of El Morya: "I have need of a feminine messenger. Go to Washington and I will train you through Mark Prophet."

A New Messenger-in-Training

When the I AM Activity was no longer useful to the Brotherhood, the Bridge to Freedom was founded. However, in 1961 the Messenger of the Bridge to Freedom committed suicide. This explained El Morya's immediate need for a feminine messenger.

And so, obedient to El Morya's call, Elizabeth flew from Boston to Washington, D.C. to attend her first conference, the July conference in 1961 at the Dodge House. She was twenty-two years old at the time, and almost all who attended were middle aged or elderly, in their 50s, 60s and 70s.

Elizabeth has since related that when El Morya called her to be a messenger, he said that her decision would determine whether or not there would be an organization of the Great White Brotherhood that was active, alive, with a voice and a messenger in this century. He said that what she did would have ramifications to the Brotherhood, the government, the planet, the solar system and beyond.

God Tabor's Pine Trees

Mark related many anecdotes concerning the early days of The Summit Lighthouse during Keepers of the Flame* meetings at his quarterly conferences in Colorado Springs.

In July 1960 he held his first major conference on East 72nd Street in New York City in the sanctuary of a lovely old mansion owned by a wealthy woman.

Although she recognized that Mark was Morya's choice as messenger, this woman was disdainful of him because he did not belong to high society. He had neither the polish she had nor the wealth nor the clothes. He bought his suits at Sears Roebuck—nineteen-dollar suits, he said—because that was all he could afford.

There was a large fireplace in her mansion, and in it there was a bough from a pine tree that was faded and dry and had been left there from Christmas some months before. He could not understand why this dead branch had been left in the fireplace all that time.

During the conference El Morya delivered an address through Mark in which he said that God Tabor* was with him on the platform at that moment and was prepared to perform a service for the entire earth, directed from this sanctuary in New York.

Lord Tabor's fiat was that every pine tree upon earth, at that moment, should exude an intensified fragrance that would saturate the earth with a purifying action.

He was charging the pine trees with a special quality of spirituality that would penetrate and purify the intellect of mankind. The master said that many would find their intellect expanding tremendously. (Drug usage was becoming a problem for our young people in the early 1960s and, as a result, a veil had begun to cloud their minds.)

Mark was somewhat of a novice at taking dictations at that time, and although he knew that he had accurately reported what the master had said, he was so shocked by the promise that had just come through him that he did not know what to do. He feared that his relationship as a leader of The Summit Lighthouse was finished because people would expect this promise to be fulfilled momentarily.

Refreshments were served after the dictation and Mark was in a state of absolute panic, wondering what he could possibly do to rectify the situation. Suddenly a woman screamed, "It's happening! It's happening!"

Lo and behold, what was happening was that in the fireplace the dead pine branch that had been cut the year before was pouring out sap (Mark said like a volcano on Hawaii) and the odor of pine was filling the room. He was tremendously relieved to see God Tabor's promise fulfilled before his very eyes.

Conferences Held at the Dodge House

At that time, Mark was responsible for all the preparations for the conference himself, even planning the altar décor. A couple of days before the class he could be seen in his overalls, cleaning the floor in the rented room, putting up the masters' pictures, the thoughtform of the class and all the other details. And then, when the day of the conference arrived, Mark would be in his suit or robe, delivering the word of God.

The Dodge House is torn down now, but for several years conferences and special meetings were held there.

The Davidson Printing Press

When Elizabeth came to The Summit Lighthouse in 1961, there were no published dictations, no bound volumes of the weekly letters from the masters known as the *Pearls of Wisdom*.* In fact, there were only three or four years of *Pearls*.

For several years, Mark received the *Pearls of Wisdom* as dictations from the ascended masters and typed them himself until Elizabeth came into the organization and purchased a dictating machine for his use. It became not only costly but also unsatisfactory to continue contracting with a printing house to publish the weekly *Pearls*. And so they purchased a Davidson printing press, which Elizabeth hid in the living room of her apartment on the tenth floor of the Arlington Towers in Virginia. She learned how to operate it and actually printed the *Pearls* herself until someone came on staff to relieve her of this function.

The Messenger Mark L. Prophet

Holy Tree House

The time came when it became more expedient to purchase a property of their own instead of renting meeting rooms and separate apartments for the staff. They also needed a home for the printing press, which Elizabeth could no longer operate in her apartment. And so, in 1962, they bought Holy Tree House in Fairfax, Virginia. It was a small little one-story building with a basement. The sanctuary was in a basement room of Holy Tree House. There were also small offices—one for Mark, one for Elizabeth, and a place for their printing press.

The Brotherhood of Gethsemane

In a dictation from Jesus in London, Ontario, Canada in 1962, Mark was asked to form a spiritual order called The Brotherhood of Gethsemane. Jesus said that it was to be in memory of those angels who ministered to him in the garden of Gethsemane before the day of his crucifixion. (Matt. 26:36–57)

Those who wished to volunteer for this service were asked to offer daily prayers and decrees for the freedom of those souls who were trapped in the astral* realm. Mark said that Jesus told him that the pain and suffering of the world could be relieved by medical science. "But," Jesus asked him, "who will relieve the pain that results from the misuse of free will when man is trapped in the astral as a result of a sudden accident, suicide, or something like that?"

The activity of this holy brotherhood was to be one of comfort—the healing branch of The Summit Lighthouse. We still have on our altars today a crystal chalice in which we place requests for healing that have come to us by letter and by telephone from all around the world. We hold a healing service every Wednesday evening worldwide called, "Watch With Me" Jesus' Vigil of the Hours.

A large part of our service includes prayers for those who have recently passed from the screen of life and may be temporarily trapped in the astral plane.* We ask holy angels to contact these souls wherever they may be, to comfort them and to escort them to their proper place in the realms of light—either for a period of rest, if they have passed in great pain or trauma, or to temples of learning where they may be prepared for their next embodiment.

1963—The Year of Changes

The year of 1963 saw many changes. The Summit Lighthouse was incorporated in the State of Delaware. The messengers and some staff traveled to Los Angeles for their first conference on the West Coast. They chose the Friday Morning

Club for their meetings and spoke there for years.

When Elizabeth arrived in Washington, Mark had told her, "I will not be here for long. I have only one thing left to do and that is to transfer the mantle of the prophet, of the messenger, to you. And when that is accomplished, you will not see me any longer."

After a period of intensive training for her, Mark and Elizabeth were married on March 16, 1963, in Annapolis, Maryland. They were together for a twelve-year cycle, from 1961 to 1973, giving forth the teachings, publishing books and tapes, holding conferences around the world, and becoming the parents of four children.

Mark's People-to-People Tour

In October, 1964, Mark Prophet took off in his little green Saab on a two-month-long people-to-people tour of the United States. His goal was to meet as many students of the ascended masters as he could contact. With a new staff member, Erwin Arndt, he traveled 14,000 miles on his tour, covering the entire United States from east to west and north to south.

His plan was to assemble three to ten or more interested people in their homes for a spiritual seminar and hopefully to start a Summit Lighthouse group in each city. In this way he contacted everyone whom he could on the mailing list.

The mailing list for the entire organization was stored in one shoe box and later expanded to two boxes—long before the days of personal computers.

Beacon's Head

After a few years, Holy Tree House was sold for a profit and The Summit Lighthouse moved to a larger property, also in Virginia, called Beacon's Head. They occupied this home for ten months and again sold it for a considerable profit. This enabled them to move to La Tourelle, their focus in Colorado Springs, Colorado.

La Tourelle

The masters realized that we needed a more central location in the United States. We needed to give our members a quicker route from all areas of the country. They wanted to give everyone an opportunity to be able to come to The Summit and attend the quarterly conferences. A large percentage of people interested in new-age teachings and metaphysics lived in California and the West.

They found a beautiful brick mansion, a Tudor property— a Shakespearean castle, as Mark described it. The house was situated on about two acres of land, beautifully landscaped, next door to the Broadmoor Hotel in Colorado Springs, which was a prime location.

Mark said that the property was El Morya's, but Saint Germain was instrumental in assisting Morya in securing this property. On every corner of the house was the seal of Saint Germain—a fleur-de-lis engraved on all the gutters.

La Tourelle was built in 1933 at a cost of several million dollars, and even in 1965 the cost was more than this young organization could afford. And yet, the property was ideal for The Summit's purpose.

It provided space for all the necessary aspects of publishing the teachings, holding quarterly seminars and worship services. It had secretarial offices and housing for an expanding staff. It was the perfect focus for an ascended master activity.

Mark told the realtor that, no matter how much they wanted the property, unless the price was cut in half, they could not purchase it. Mark and Elizabeth had flown out to Colorado Springs from Beacon's Head in Virginia and had only been back home for a few days when they received a phone call from the realtors. The owner had agreed to cut the price in half! And thus, Morya got his focus at La Tourelle.

Elizabeth was eight months pregnant with their second child at Christmas 1965. She flew out to Colorado Springs while Mark and the staff packed up the printing press and their

Mark Prophet in his office at La Tourelle

other possessions and drove out West. There followed an intense period of relocating and completely redecorating while still carrying on the day-to-day duties, including the weekly publishing of the *Pearls of Wisdom.*

The Easter Class of 1966 was held in the beautiful sanctuary, newly painted white and gold.

Elizabeth said, "We are at a position now either to expand or we cease to be. That is the law of cosmos.* You have to keep on transcending yourself. If you try to remain at a certain static point, you die for lack of growth. A plant cannot remain in a certain place. It either grows more leaves or it dies." The Summit Lighthouse continued to expand in Colorado Springs from 1966 until 1973, when we moved our headquarters to Santa Barbara, California. We continued our publishing activities at La Tourelle until 1977.

CHAPTER FOUR

MEETING MARK PROPHET

My Trip Around the World

Before I proceed with my narrative, I think it is time for me to tell you how I met Mark Prophet. My husband and I owned a photographic studio in Hayward, California. The professional photographers group to which we belonged contracted with a reputable travel agent for a trip around the world. I had always had an unfulfilled wish for travel and this provided an excellent opportunity for me to travel with professional friends.

I paid my deposit and we were scheduled to depart on July 5, 1966. However, to my amazement, on May 31, I received a phone call saying that the most surprising event had transpired. I was the *only one* of all the professional photographers in the United States who had actually paid the deposit and so they had to cancel the tour. They said that this had never happened before in their entire history of booking tours.

However, they assured me that they had another trip leaving soon and would like me to accompany that group. I agreed because I really wanted to travel around the world. (Overseas travel was not as commonplace then as it is now.) As it turned out, the original tour was scheduled to arrive at each of the locations where the ascended masters have their retreats*—India, Ceylon, Paris, Crete, Germany, Egypt. I had never heard of the teachings at that time, but I have since wondered if perhaps it was the radiation of the masters' retreats that drew me to this trip.

As the time drew near for departure, I began to feel that I was not supposed to go. It became very embarrassing because my friends were arranging good-bye showers for me. It was quite an event in those days in our small town for someone to travel around the world. My refusal to go even created friction with my husband because he was afraid people would think his wife could not afford the trip. Nevertheless, I stood true to my intuition that told me not to go. So finally the day of departure arrived, and I remained at home—in a rather bad mood, you can imagine—because I could think of no reason why I should not go.

About a month later, as I was burning old newspapers in the fireplace, I read that on the very day when I would have arrived in India, the monsoons had started early and the very city where I would have been that day was flooded. Another Indian town on our itinerary was rioting because the government had begun to use contraceptives on the cows roaming all over India. The priests and monks were rioting because they lacked enough dung to burn in the lamps in the temples. The trip would have been a disaster!

When I met Mark Prophet later, I told him about my trip around the world that never materialized and that just as soon as I had given it up, I found an invitation to The Summit Lighthouse. He said that everyone must make their search for the masters, and this was my way of searching, even though I knew nothing about the masters or their retreats in my outer mind. He said that my soul knew, though, and that I had actually contacted the masters through my desire to make the trip.

In succeeding years, I was fortunate enough to travel with Mark and Elizabeth and the ascended masters to each of the locations on my proposed itinerary and more. It was much more rewarding to travel with a group of spiritual seekers than it would have been with professional photographers.

Finding The Summit Lighthouse

We had built a successful wedding photography business in Hayward, California, across the bay from San Francisco. Of course, brides get married on Saturdays and Sundays.

Since I could no longer attend our Methodist church on the weekends, I still felt the need for some spirituality in my life. I had a very fundamentalist upbringing until my marriage when I joined the Methodist Church.

I began reading the publications from Unity and would send my tithes to Silent Unity, their prayer group. Each month, as a receipt, they would send an affirmation such as, "The Christ Mind is blessing and prospering me now," or something similar. You were supposed to repeat this all month as your affirmation of prosperity.

One month I received an unusual response: "Jesus Christ is here now." I ran back to the dark room in our photo studio and showed it to my husband. He said, "No, this is just an affirmation of the Christ Mind." My reply was, "Oh no, it really means what it says: 'Jesus Christ is here now.' "

I knew that this affirmation meant exactly what it said, and I was determined to find out what it meant. I phoned my sister, who was aware of all the psychic movements at the moment, and asked her if she had heard anything about Jesus being here now. I asked her to be especially vigilant because I was convinced that I had received that affirmation for a reason.

A few days later I received a phone call from her: "Annice, I have your answer! I received a message from Jesus and he is inviting you to have lunch with him in the garden."

She had answered an advertisement in *Fate* magazine placed by Carol Hudspeth that read, "Saint Germain wants you!" And when she wrote to find out about it, she received an invitation from The Summit Lighthouse in Colorado Springs for their Harvest Conference. It read, "Jesus is inviting you to have lunch with him in the garden."

My immediate response was, "Oh, this is what my affirmation means." My sister said, "Wait, it gets better! I have a *letter* from Jesus too." She was laughing as she began to read one of the Corona Class Lessons from the early *Pearls of Wisdom.**

I recognized Jesus' vibration immediately and said, "Stop laughing. This is authentic. It really *is* Jesus. I'm going to come over right away." I put a sign on the door of our photo studio that we were closed for half an hour, got in my car and zoomed over to my sister's house. She still thought it was a big joke, but I did not mind because now I had really found Jesus. My sister wasn't interested in the invitation, but it was through her and *Fate* magazine and the ad, "Saint Germain wants you!" that I found the masters, The Summit Lighthouse and Mark Prophet.

The Harvest Class, October 1966

Now that I had received an invitation from Jesus, I certainly intended to go but had no idea how that was possible. We had not had a vacation for years due to the demands of our business, but I was determined to use all the psychology and salesmanship I possessed to convince my husband to go to Colorado Springs. I knew he enjoyed photography and told him that Colorado must be beautiful in the autumn. I was determined to go myself but preferred to go with my husband.

In the meantime I had ordered a few books from The Summit Lighthouse and realized from a book called "Overcoming Fear Through Decrees" by Lord Maitreya that we would be decreeing during the conference. This book explained that decrees are a form of high frequency energy and very effective prayer. I waited until we had almost arrived in Colorado Springs before I showed my husband the book. I did not want him to turn around and go back home.

When I first walked into La Tourelle, I did not know what to expect—whether I would find a swami with a turban or someone with a crystal ball or what. I had no idea as to what the ascended masters were, but I felt compelled to find out.

On the first afternoon, at the close of the vespers service, Mark shook hands with us at the door. I knew nothing about radiation at the time, but I know that if I had not been near enough to grab the doorknob to steady myself, my knees would have buckled. This was my introduction to Mark Prophet.

On the first day of the conference there had been a snow storm, a blizzard so serious that planes couldn't arrive. (Of course, we had driven in the day before the storm so we could take some photographs.) There couldn't have been more than twenty or twenty-five devotees in the sanctuary that first night. Communion had been scheduled.

I had worn a very stylish pumpkin-colored knit suit, the latest thing in San Francisco at the moment. And my husband wore his black suit that he always wore to photograph weddings. So here we were—an island of orange and black surrounded by everyone else in pastels. My comment was, "These women's clothes would never be accepted in San Francisco."

Elizabeth said, "Now, we are having Communion at our service tonight. If you are asking what is acceptable to wear, we recommend white, preferably, or pastel pink or blue." Back at the motel I said, "You know, I don't think she likes my suit." Since I had no pastels in my suitcase, I decided to wear my brown wool dress and, of course, my husband wore his black suit again.

So there we sat, this conspicuous island of brown and black sitting in the midst of everyone in white (even the men) when Communion was served. And that is how I learned about the ascended master's choice of colors—the hard way. (The masters recommend pastel colors whenever possible.) The moment each of us saw Mark and Elizabeth, we knew instantly that this movement was authentic and that they truly were messengers of God. When I walked in the front door of La Tourelle, I realized that my whole life belonged now and forevermore to the Brotherhood.

Since there was such a small attendance at the Harvest Class because of the extreme weather, we were given a chance to know the messengers personally in a way that could not have been possible if there had been a larger attendance. We took them and their family to dinner several times during the class and were able to ask many questions about the teachings. The depth of information we received personally from the messengers as well as the class lectures and dictations were a great blessing and an eye-opener to me. I have never forgotten my first conference at La Tourelle and my first impressions of Mark and Elizabeth Prophet.

CHAPTER FIVE

GLIMPSES OF THE ADEPT: MARK'S TRIP TO HAYWARD

Turning Back a California Earthquake

In September, 1967, Mark visited our home in Hayward. He said he was sent by the Brotherhood on an emergency mission to try to avoid a major earthquake scheduled for Northern California.

Since I was a member of the San Francisco Study Group at that time, he instructed me to call an emergency meeting of as many members as I could contact. He would try to receive a dictation from one of the masters and hopefully turn aside the predicted earthquake.

We held a meeting in the Marines' Memorial Building in San Francisco, and Vaivasvata Manu* dictated that evening. We were told that as a result, the earthquake had been averted from our area.

Haight-Ashbury

In the '60s the Haight-Ashbury district of San Francisco was becoming known as a haven for "hippies" and "flower children." Mark was particularly concerned about the use of drugs that was popular there and which has become a major problem for our youth since then.

He said that he would like to see if he could do some spiritual work to help the situation. He asked if he could borrow our little 1966 Mustang convertible that he loved to drive whenever he had a chance. Since Mark was accustomed to

Portrait taken at Les Booth Photography, Hayward, California 1967.

driving big vans and buses and station wagons, our little sports car was a special treat for him.

On his way over to Haight-Ashbury, Mark stopped in at our photographic studio and my husband took his portrait. We have since printed it in several of our books.

Since he had been our guest for several days, I thought he might be tired of my cooking, and so I suggested that we go downtown to a small restaurant owned by my friend. It was an unusually hot day for that time of year and the air conditioning was most welcome.

As we were leaving the restaurant, a blast of hot air hit us and I exclaimed, "Oh, how I wish we could take this air conditioning with us."

As we were walking to our car, I suddenly began to shiver and broke out in "goose bumps." Mark paid no attention until

I said, "Mark, what are you doing to me?" He answered, "Well, you said you wished you could take the air conditioning with you." And I said, "Well, please turn it off! I'm freezing." I was beginning to realize some of the attainment he had as an adept.

As he was driving me back to my home, Mark said, "Oh, I would love to turn this traffic light to green, but I promised Morya I wouldn't do it again." When I asked what he meant, he related to me the time when he got in trouble with Morya about traffic lights.

He said that he was in a big hurry to get someplace and every single light turned red just as he approached it. Knowing full well the laws of energy, Mark just zapped that light. It, as well as the ones for blocks ahead, turned green—and created the most horrendous traffic snarl you could ever imagine.

Fortunately there were no injuries, but El Morya appeared to him and told him sternly, "Mark you have to abide by the physical laws in the physical octave." So, the next light he came to that turned red—he stopped.

Mark had the attainment and powers of an adept, and yet since he was in a physical body in a Western country, he was also bound by the laws of the land.

About two weeks after Mark returned to Colorado Springs, a major San Francisco newspaper printed an article entitled, "Where have all the 'flower children' gone?" It stated that for some unknown reason many of the young people on drugs were leaving San Francisco. (Well, of course, we knew why they had left, since Mark had walked the streets of Haight-Ashbury.)

Mark's Teaching to My Father

I asked one favor of Mark before he returned home. I had been trying to explain the teachings of the ascended masters to my family and so far seemed to have had no results. I was especially close to my elderly father and wanted to be sure that he knew about Saint Germain before he passed.

My father had been a heart patient for many years. We lived in Denver, Colorado in 1930, and the doctor said that if we went to either coast he could probably live six months, but he was going to die within six weeks if he stayed in Denver. So we moved to Los Angeles, and he passed away in 1968. His six months was extended to 38 years!

My father was a devout man, a good Christian. I had an orthodox upbringing. We always went to the most fundamental church, whatever denomination it was, wherever we moved. My father was very close to Jesus and I thought, "Well, when he finds out about the masters, he's going to move right along with us."

I spent many hours explaining the teachings to him, but because of his fundamentalist beliefs he could not understand reincarnation. When I found that Mark Prophet was coming to visit, I increased the tempo of explaining the teachings to my father because I had decided that he must be ready. I could see no reason why, since he loved Jesus, that he would not accept the other masters.

When Mark arrived, I said, "May I please have a barbecue tonight? I'll invite my father and all my family and *you* explain the teachings to them." I had spent two years trying to explain reincarnation and felt there must be just one sentence that I was not saying correctly. Mark consented and explained the entire teachings of the ascended masters to my family—basically and simply.

My father had recently been in the hospital and by eleven o'clock that evening I knew that he had to go to bed. I said, "Now, Daddy, do you understand?" And he said, "Oh, yes, this is beautiful! But, Mark, I want to ask you one more question before I go home.

"My daughter said that you were Mark in the Bible, and that is my favorite book. But how could you have written that and be sitting here tonight in my daughter's backyard?" Mark just put his arms around him and said, "Go to bed, dear heart. God bless you."

But Mark took me aside and gave me a stern lecture. He said, "Young lady, you leave your father alone. He's a very good man and he's very close to Jesus. He has excellent karma; he has been following the path that he took embodiment on. He vowed he would uphold Jesus' church and he has. The fact that he doesn't know Saint Germain is not going to hurt him in the least. His soul knows."

He told me to tell my father that the next time he's not feeling well, all he has to do is say, "Father, into thy hands I commend my spirit," and Jesus will take him. About six weeks later he was in the hospital again and I said, "Daddy, I want to tell you something Mark told me," and gave him Mark's instructions. My father then said, "You mean I'm not going to hell?" I said, "No, you're not going to hell." The next day he passed.

Mark wanted me to know that there are many elderly people whose mission this lifetime may not be to follow Saint Germain and the ascended masters. The fact that my father was working with Jesus up until the last minute means that perhaps on the inner he knew all about the teachings that I was trying to explain to him. These old Pisceans will come back as new little Aquarians and hopefully, make their ascension. They don't need to know and accept karma and reincarnation with their physical minds in this lifetime because their souls know these truths on inner levels.

Cataclysmic Weather

A serious flood occurred in the Sacramento, Yuba City area a few days after Mark left the Bay Area. Property damage and loss of life were severe. I phoned Mark for an explanation. I said, "I know that this may be the karma of the area and also the individual karma of those who are suffering loss, but what good does that do if they don't know about karma?" Mark answered, "The master wants you to know that their *souls* know."

He continued to explain to me that the elemental beings* of earth, air, fire and water had been holding back cataclysm and taking into their own little bodies, as it were, the misqualified energy that mankind had been spewing forth—anger, hatred, frustration, fear and other negative emotions.

Mark explained that the masters had predicted vast and sweeping changes in the weather over the nation and the world. They predicted that whatever negativity mankind sent forth would now be returned to them because the nature spirits, or elementals, were no longer required to absorb this malevolence. He said it was very uncomfortable for the elementals to hold this energy within their forms and that they are no longer required to do so.

The elementals keep taking in energy just as you would wind up a spring and then build up force enough on certain occasions to then uncoil all that energy as a hurricane, flood, forest fire or catastrophe of some sort. The masters have said that whenever possible, the children of the light would be protected from this uncoiling manifestation of negative energy. This teaching can certainly explain much of the unusual weather patterns we are experiencing at present.

I can't begin to remember all the times I bothered Mark with my questions and all the wonderful answers I received. I have been most fortunate to know Mark Prophet as a physical man as well as an adept and now also as the Ascended Master Lanello.

CHAPTER SIX

EUROPE

MARK DECIDED THAT ELIZABETH needed a "rest" after the birth of their third child. I am putting "rest" in quotation marks because I soon found out that a messenger's idea of a rest was not equivalent to my definition of the word.

He invited me to accompany them to Europe, although I was fairly new to the teachings and not yet a member of The Summit Lighthouse staff. Of course, I gladly accepted because I realized that this trip could be a replacement for the around-the-world trip that I had surrendered earlier.

We planned a six-weeks tour of Europe and booked reservations on the S.S. Bremen and return on the S.S. United States. Mark, Elizabeth, their three children—Sean four years, Erin two years and Moira eight months—Ruth Jones, Tom Miller, three other members of the organization and I boarded the ship at New York on August 3, 1968.

No reservations for our tour were made through a travel agent. Elizabeth's mother, Fridy Wulf, was to meet us in Germany and conduct us around Europe. This sounded very simple as we made our plans! Nothing was paid in advance except the steamship fares—no nightly reservations at inns, no food, no gasoline for our van. I soon learned the obstacles and projections faced by the messengers in their daily lives that were accepted as usual occurrences.

I took $2,000 out of our saving account for my initial expenses and told my husband that I would wire him for more as I needed it. However, for safety's sake, I only took $1,000 in travelers checks with me and fully expected to wire for more from time to time during our six-weeks tour.

Aboard the S.S. Bremen

Mark assured me that the fare we had paid included all our food and snacks aboard ship. However, it was necessary for me to watch my food intake even though it was already prepaid. I had been constantly fighting overweight since my thyroid surgery twenty years before.

The first morning at breakfast Mark told me that I could order anything I wanted and proceeded to enjoy a huge breakfast himself. However, I had my normal breakfast: a Dexedrine pill and a cup of tea. Mark was appalled. He said, "Mrs. Booth, that's not what you do on a ship. You have already paid for everything."

For lunch I had another diet pill, a cup of bouillon and a

Aboard the S.S Bremen enroute to Europe

green salad. Dinner was my third Dexedrine pill of the day, a broiled lamb chop and a few steamed vegetables. Mark said, "Well, all I have to say is *you are no fun!* I thought when I invited you to come along that I was going to have fun with you." I answered, "Mark, it is impossible for me to eat the quantity of food most people do. You can see that I am overweight now and this is how I have eaten for the last several years of my life just to maintain my present weight."

He didn't say anything and continued to enjoy his steaks, roast duck and delicious calorie-laden meals. (We were not vegetarians at that time.) And I continued my Dexedrine pills and bouillon and green salad for the duration of the time aboard the Bremen.

Mark's Attunement with the Elementals

We disembarked from the ship in Bremerhaven, Germany in an absolute downpour. Mark had rented a Volkswagen van for us to tour Europe in and had also ordered a new one to be picked up at the factory. He planned to use this second one for his family's car and also to ship it back home for use at The Summit Lighthouse later.

But in the meantime, until he took ownership of his new VW, we were all crowded into this one rented van. We had to put all our luggage on the roof but were unable to find a tarpaulin in the entire city. There was nothing to do but to start traveling and hope that the rain would not ruin our luggage.

Since we had no reservations for that night, it took quite a while to find an inn with vacancies enough for this many people. In the meantime, our luggage was getting drenched.

All of a sudden from the front seat, I heard the words, "Peace, be still." I have never experienced such love in my entire life as was contained in just those three little words. The rain stopped instantly. No one seemed to have noticed Mark's command to the elementals except me. Eventually someone in the car said, "Oh, look, it stopped raining!" No one seemed to have realized the impact of what Mark had accomplished in love.

My Sudden Weight Loss

We did not mention my eating habits again until a couple of days later when Mark, Elizabeth, Sean and I were on a train on our way to the factory to pick up the new Volkswagen bus he had ordered. We left the rest of the group behind with the other children.

Mark happened to be sitting across the aisle from me on the train and asked, "What do you think is the problem with your weight, Mrs. Booth?" My answer was, "My thyroid gland, which regulates metabolism, was surgically removed." No more was said on this matter.

The next morning in our little German inn, Mark knocked on my door and said, "Open the door. I want to look at you." I couldn't imagine what was going on. The second morning he repeated the same process. On the third morning he knocked on the door and said, "Mrs. Booth, do you realize your clothes don't fit anymore? They are just hanging on you." Well, I had not realized, but I remembered, then, that I had taken a safety pin that day to hold up my skirt.

When he said, "Now, will you eat with me?" I suddenly realized the great adept with whom we were traveling. In those three days I had lost twenty-five pounds and I have no idea how many inches.

And yes, believe me, I ate as I had not been able to eat in years. I ate wherever we went all over Europe, everything you can imagine, including those beautiful, gooey, delicious pastries for which Germany and Scandinavia are famous. And apparently I was finally the fun that Mark had expected me to be when he invited me.

My sudden weight loss created quite a stir when we again joined the group. And my husband couldn't believe his eyes when I arrived home on the plane.

I realized that weight is more than counting calories and eating a low fat or high-carbohydrate diet. The visualization of an adept with powers like Mark Prophet was more valuable than any diet pills could ever be. I told him that if he would open a weight reduction salon, he would be more financially successful than Elizabeth Arden and have plenty of money to expand The Summit Lighthouse. His answer was that Saint Germain would not allow him to capitalize on his yogic powers for commercial gain, and he would probably lose his attainment if he misused it.

Mark said that Saint Germain had allowed him to help me because my karma merited it at that moment. Apparently it must have been remission of karma, because Mark was able to keep my excess weight off until he ascended. But after that I began to gain again while still eating the same food as before and following the same regimen.

The Bishop of Bingen's Mouse Tower on the Rhine

We traveled all over Germany and Switzerland in our two buses. It was impossible to maintain any type of schedule with three young children. We often stopped along the road and made our lunch of soup and sandwiches. This gave the children a chance to run and play for a few minutes and also gave us a chance to implement our cash outlay for the day.

As we were driving along the Rhine River, enjoying the exquisite beauty of the scenery, Mark suddenly cried, "Oh, there's my mouse tower on the Rhine!" I thought I had better keep quiet because I had no idea what the "mouse tower on the Rhine" was. He said, "Mrs. Booth, did not you read Longfellow's *Children's Hour* where he mentions the Bishop of Bingen and his mouse tower on the Rhine?" Mark said the radiation was so strong that he could recognize the focus immediately. I wouldn't be at all surprised if Bingen on the Rhine is the location of Lanello's retreat, because I know it is somewhere over the Rhine in Germany.

Opening a Swiss Bank Account

Elizabeth had a cousin in Switzerland who was a beautician. While they were renewing their acquaintance, Mark asked me to accompany him to a Swiss bank in Geneva. When we arrived at the cashier's window, Mark said, "All right, Mrs. Booth, talk French." I hadn't spoken a word of French since my college days thirty years before.

(It seemed that one of Mark's dreams had always been to have a numbered Swiss bank account, and he planned to open it with *five dollars!*) While I stumbled around trying desperately to remember any French, the man said, "Madam, would you like me to speak English?" That saved me the embarrassment of my French and also having to explain that we wanted to open a numbered account for *five dollars!* Mark could now do the talking himself in English.

In the Swiss Alps

Elizabeth had attended school in Switzerland during her junior year in high school. (She had numerous Swiss relatives with whom she stayed and with whom she traveled throughout Europe.) She was especially thrilled with the beauty of the Swiss Alps and couldn't wait to acquaint Mark and me with their magnificence. One day we were traveling in our Volkswagen bus up a mountainous road in the Alps but could see absolutely nothing. The entire area was blanketed in a dense fog.

She appealed to Mark several times to use his ability to command the elementals to change the weather patterns. He answered her that he could do nothing this time. Elizabeth was disappointed because we were unable to see any of the beauty surrounding us, and so she started to call to Astrea,* hoping to clear the fog and reverse the tide of opposition to our trip. After about a half hour El Morya said to Mark, "Tell Elizabeth to continue her decrees. It is good for her soul, but it will not change the weather today."

Mark later explained that the masters had deliberately invoked that fog as a protection for us against the false hierarchy* who had their retreat* in the Alps. We proceeded to our destination on the Rigi near Lucerne and returned, but never for a moment were we able to catch a glimpse of the Swiss Alps.

Precipitating Money

At another time, somewhere in Europe—I don't remember the town—we went to a small bank to exchange our travelers checks for the currency of the country. I noticed that my book of checks still felt heavy although we had been in Europe for several weeks, paying for our inns every night, renting a car, buying food, gas and all the sundry expenses of the trip. I had also begun to pay many of the expenses for the Prophet family and had fully expected to wire home several times before now for more money.

Mark saw the look of puzzlement on my face and said, "Count your travelers checks, Mrs. Booth." To my amazement I had spent only two hundred dollars in all these weeks. That was my first experience of the masters precipitating money in my wallet. Mark said that they could do this because I had been generous with my money and had not spent it on trinkets for myself.

We continued our trip and I was paying for myself and also many of the Prophets' expenses. When we returned to New York, a city where I had never been before, I went on a shopping spree buying gifts for others and myself. I still arrived home with $400 of the original $1,000 in travelers checks. I realized that it was absolutely impossible to travel in Europe as we had for six weeks and also shop in New York City for only $600. I felt that this was precipitated money that did not belong to me. I immediately sent a check to The Summit Lighthouse.

The days of Jesus' miracles are still with us!

Rome: St. Peter's and the Vatican

We took a fast train down to Rome. I had been a Latin major in college and had always wanted to visit Rome and especially St. Peter's Cathedral and the Vatican. And yet, standing in this beautiful Cathedral, I felt no radiation at all, no flame. I was heartbroken. Mark came up to me and said, "Mrs. Booth, what is the matter?" I said, "Mark, there must be something wrong with me. Maybe I'm just too tired, but I don't feel anything here." And he answered, "No, dear heart, there is no radiation here now."

About that time a little Italian man in a beautiful silk suit came up and said, "I would like to take you on a tour of Rome today." And Mark said, "Absolutely." By this time I was paying for the entire trip and said, "Wait a minute!" Mark said, "Be still. This is Morya's man."

We traveled all over Rome and it was just glorious—just as I had always dreamed. Our guide took us to the Forum and the Coliseum, and as I was standing there, just enraptured with the ruins, he said, "Little lady, you love Rome, don't you?" I answered, "Oh, I love Rome, but I am so disappointed with the Vatican." He answered, "Don't worry, I have something special planned for you today."

Quo Vadis

Our guide took us to a little church called Quo Vadis, which in Latin means "Where are you going? Where are you walking?" It was a tiny little building on the Via Appia, probably not more than six or eight pews. But here we found the radiation that was missing from the Vatican. There was a plaque on the floor that contained Jesus' footprint, burned in the sand as he walked along the Appian Way.

We have been told that Peter met the risen Christ on the Via Appia as Peter was fleeing Rome to avoid persecution. He asked, "Quo vadis, Domine (Lord)?" And Jesus announced, "I am going to Rome to be crucified again." Then Peter knew that it was his destiny to return to Rome and later be crucified. Mark took off his sandals and stood in Jesus' footprint, and we all knelt down and put our hands in his footprint. The radiation was almost overwhelming, even two-thousand years later. And thus, thanks to El Morya and the guide whom he sent us, we were really allowed to see Rome!

Stonehenge and Salisbury

After a stormy crossing of the English Channel, we arrived in England and were preparing for home. First, however, we spent a day at Stonehenge and Salisbury. After a delightful day spent amid the ruins of Stonehenge, we went to a lovely English Cathedral nearby at Salisbury.

Mark asked, "How do you like it here, Mrs. Booth?" My answer was, "I don't know why, but I think this is the most beautiful cathedral I have ever seen—lovelier than Rheims, Notre Dame and Chartres, which we have visited." Mark said, "Well, fine, it was yours once. You were Dame Katherine Momparnass, the lady of this manor and, by the way, there is your tomb over there." All the other tombs were white and there was this one with a woman's statue lying above the tomb. She had curly hair and was dressed in a blue robe with gold fleur-de-lis.

You were constantly coming upon your past when you were with Mark, and he didn't mind in the least telling you your past embodiments in front of anyone who happened to be around—oftentimes to your embarrassment. We weren't all saints, you know, in every lifetime. So, apparently the reason that I felt so comfortable in this beautiful cathedral was that I had been mistress of the land at one time.

The same thing occurred when we stepped down into the catacombs in Rome. I just knew that I had been there previously during the era of the early Christian Church and felt completely at home underground. Occasionally it seems that you tap into the akashic records* of a place where you have been in a previous lifetime.

Driving Through the Wall

And now it was time for dinner and we went to a lovely little British inn nearby. We parked in the parking lot with no problem—plenty of space. Since Mark did not want to bring his large VW bus, I had rented a smaller English car with the steering wheel on the right-hand side.

After our dinner we came out to the parking lot to find it much more crowded than an hour or so before. For those of you who drive, you know that when you are in a tight spot, you back up a little bit and then go forward a few feet. You do this several times until you are free. Well, Mark just kept going straight, straight, straight, very slowly. And of course, we were in my rented English car with the steering wheel on the wrong side.

I was sitting in the front seat on the side next to the wall and kept saying, "Mark! Mark! Mark!" I was not prepared to pay the expense of a rental car being ruined unnecessarily. Mark kept going straight ahead until we were up against the stones in the wall, and yet he continued going straight ahead. I kept shrinking in my shoulders because I could see we were going to hit the wall. But, for some reason we didn't! I kept listening for the noise of a collision.

Someone in the back seat said, "Oh look, we're in the wall!" I looked out my window and here we were—in the wall! The stones had absolutely moved out of our way! There was no question about it. About one half of my rental car, including myself, was in the wall of the building and the remainder of the wall continued straight up above us.

Mark said, "Please be still. This requires concentration. It is an initiation from Saint Germain and I almost failed it with your 'Mark! Mark! Mark!'" I was still in a state of shock trying to decide how much the rental agency would charge me for my car when I returned it.

Until you become accustomed to living with someone like Mark Prophet, it is a bit difficult to anticipate events like this.

There was not a scratch on the car when I returned it to the agency.

It is impossible to explain the fourth dimension in third-dimensional terms, but I have done my best to faithfully record this day in our life during our European trip.

But yes, we did drive through the wall! A Keeper of the Flame Lesson* teaches that space is full of holes. There is absolutely no problem driving through solid walls if you have an adept like Mark Prophet behind the wheel. However, I don't recommend it to you and I shouldn't care to try driving through a wall myself.

Later that evening Mark explained this event to us. He said that when he saw that his car was hemmed in, he just made up his mind that the wall wasn't there. And the wall moved right out of his way—the wall moved back, the car went right through, and then the wall went back into place. He said, "It is all a matter of belief. I just didn't believe that that wall was going to stop me."

He continued his instruction: "Matter is just like water. When you accept that concept of physical hard matter as water, you can make it move—that is if you have faith." He said that he was able to sustain that faith just long enough to turn the car around and pass through a portion of the wall.

Mark said that there are all kinds of powers residual in us. Christ used these powers constantly, as when he helped Peter walk on the water. (Matt. 14:22–33) The problem we have today is that we don't understand the mysteries because we have never studied them.

We are brought up in a world of matter—solid substance. Mark said, "We believe that the mind is just something to think with. We don't understand how we can deceive the mind and make it do things for us. We don't understand how the Spirit can direct the mind. When we do, things really begin to happen."

My European trip with the Messengers turned out to be a great blessing, a lot of fun and a needed lesson in faith.

CHAPTER SEVEN

THE MOTHERHOUSE IN SANTA BARBARA

IN 1969, THE SUMMIT LIGHTHOUSE established their second focus in Santa Barbara, California. This was to be a retreat called the Motherhouse of the Keepers of the Flame Fraternity.

The Motherhouse was important to the masters' plan for the expansion of the activity. First, it must provide a suitable base of operations for our expanding California and West Coast membership. We had many members in California, especially in the Los Angeles area, who could attend functions much more often in Santa Barbara than in Colorado Springs.

And second, this focus was a point of contact central to Los Angeles and San Francisco and yet removed from the concentration and density of the large cities. Santa Barbara was a place where we could look out to sea and yet gaze backward upon the mountains. Truly, "America the beautiful!"

In Mark's own words: "At present the grass is green and beautiful, the sea is calm, the scent of sweet flowers is in the air and the birds are singing. Santa Barbara has a character all of its own."

The Motherhouse was located on Santa Barbara Street, near the famous Santa Barbara Mission. Most tourists going to the Mission would need to pass our focus. All in all, it was an excellent location for the ascended masters' plans for the future.

Joining Staff

My husband and I had planned on joining the staff for several months. This presented a good opportunity for us to close our business in our photographic studio in Northern California and move to Santa Barbara, a city we had always loved and planned as a residence for our retirement. We joined the staff of The Summit Lighthouse in March, 1969. I wouldn't have missed one minute of life on staff, but I must say it did have its challenges and wasn't exactly my idea of retirement.

Montecito

The original plan when The Summit Lighthouse moved to Santa Barbara was to purchase a lovely mansion in Montecito, a wealthy suburb of Santa Barbara. The Health Department and Planning Commission had already approved our use of this property. However, we still needed approval by the Montecito Protective Association. Many of the neighbors who owned property surrounding our proposed focus were adamantly opposed to having a religious activity in their neighborhood.

We felt that there should be no problem since there was a gate and high hedge surrounding the property and plenty of off-street parking on the property. We planned to hold two conferences per year there and move a small staff out to Santa Barbara to keep the records of the Keepers of the Flame Fraternity.

My husband and I, Dr. Helen MacDonald and several others, as well as Mark and Elizabeth, attended the zoning meeting in Montecito. The stipulations under which they were willing to grant us use of the property were absolutely unacceptable to us and would curtail our plans for a Santa Barbara focus.

Their demands were: We could buy the house. The Prophet family could live there personally with one secretary and domestic staff. We could only hold one conference of two days duration per year with only one hundred attendees. They would also allow occasional prayer groups of thirty persons.

Naturally we withdrew our purchase offer because this was not our vision for Santa Barbara. The masters had wanted a focus of light in Santa Barbara that would be a buffer between the darkness rampant in Los Angeles and San Francisco at that time.

Temple B'nai Brith

However, the ascended masters always seem to have an alternate plan. Since we had driven down from San Francisco and Mark and Elizabeth had come out from Colorado Springs, the realtor asked if she could show us another property before we went home.

She said, "There is one more place I could show you. It is a Jewish Synagogue called Temple B'nai Brith. They are building a new one out in the suburbs. Of course, it is rather run down, but I think you might be able to use it." Well, we took a look at what was to become the Motherhouse. It was the dirtiest place I had ever seen in my life. Hunks of plaster were even falling off the walls.

Elizabeth said, "Oh no, we couldn't buy anything like this." I certainly agreed with her. Mark just groaned and said, "I hate to tell you, but I think Morya can use this. The reason I'm sure is because there is a lion embossed on the fountain." Of course, Mark was called the Lion of Saint Mark from his embodiment as the Gospel writer. He said, "I think this is Morya's place."

Since I was to be the director of the Motherhouse, I said, "Mark, I just can't do it." He answered, "Well, you are going to have to because this is Morya's place." And thus began my life as the "housemother" of the Motherhouse—my official title.

As we were leaving Santa Barbara that night for home— rather discouraged, I might say—a huge oil slick began to spread over the ocean and beach in Montecito. Many of the very ones who had refused to allow us to buy property in Montecito owned beachfront resorts and businesses there. There were incredible monetary loses that year as the oil killed fish, wildlife and polluted the beaches. Mark said that the masters told him that this tragedy came upon Santa Barbara as a response of the elementals to Montecito's rejection of the light.

And so, on March 18, 1969, we acquired title to "Synagogue B'nai Brith," a sizable building located on almost two acres of land. This property, originally the home of an executive of the Santa Fe Railroad, was centrally located in the midst of the city, about two blocks from the Santa Barbara Mission and already zoned for church use. (We were taking no chances this time.)

Although the building was badly in need of renovation, it would eventually provide a suitable home for the masters' purposes. There would be space for a chapel, reading room, offices, formal and informal activities and classrooms for a small college—the beginning of our Ascended Master University.

Remodeling the Motherhouse

While a crew of four men tackled the huge task of painting and rebuilding the focus, I soon found what my part was to be. I had laughed when Mark told me that I was to be the housemother of the Motherhouse. He said, "Don't laugh. Soon enough you will find out what that title entails." And that was an understatement! I soon found that my assignment included bookkeeping and administrative duties, purchasing food, cooking meals, cleaning house, supervising staff, conducting services and doing whatever was needed to get the job done.

In addition, I often worked in two locations, commuting between cities. I flew back and forth between Santa Barbara and La Tourelle, still The Summit Lighthouse Headquarters in Colorado Springs, to help Mark and Elizabeth complete the book *Climb The Highest Mountain.*

Archangel Michael's Protection

Those of us on staff at the Motherhouse soon learned the meaning of obedience in a very tangible way in those early days. Everything had to be taken apart and redone in order to make the synagogue into a beautiful ascended master focus. At one time we had all five large glass doors opening onto the formal lawn down at the mill being reworked. We had almost every window in the place out and at the shop.

I was concerned about security and called back to La Tourelle and said, "Mark, how do I lock up this place?" He told us that Archangel Michael said, "If you will do your decrees every night, post a guard every night without fail, be certain to lock every door that is still on the Motherhouse and lock every window that is still in place, my blue flame angels will protect the rest." And that was the truth. We had absolutely no vandalism even though the property was very open.

Can you imagine going around and locking two doors very carefully when five or six of them were open, covered only by plastic sheeting? And just how silly would you feel, every night, carefully locking maybe six or seven windows when all the rest of the openings were gaping holes? But we did it faithfully for about a month. And in the process we learned a valuable lesson in faith and trust. We found that we had Archangel Michael as our protection and he never failed us.

And so, we completely redid the entire area and made it truly an ascended master focus. We sandblasted the outside of the building and painted it a sparkling white with small gold chips that gleamed in the sun. It was rapidly becoming a "House of Light."

The Master El Morya Walking the Property

At one time before we opened the focus for the public, we received a nice surprise. We couldn't hold any services or public decree sessions because the property was in such a state of disrepair. There were only four or five staff and most of the time I was at La Tourelle working on the book.

During one of those times when I was at La Tourelle, Mark

said, "Saint Germain says we need more light in Santa Barbara." So we all piled in his motor home and drove out. On the way he told us that Saint Germain intended to give his first dictation in the Motherhouse in order to raise the vibration. Of course, we were thrilled—our first dictation in the Motherhouse!

We chose the least torn-up room in the place, and Saint Germain began his dictation through Mark. The Master said, "And now, while I am speaking, Master El Morya is physically walking the property." Well, we could scarcely care what Saint Germain said after that. All we wanted to do was get out and see El Morya.

And Saint Germain talked, and he talked, and he talked. To this day I can't tell you what he said. And we wiggled, and we wiggled, and we wiggled. And finally, after an interminable period of time, or so it seemed, Saint Germain said, "Alright, Master Morya has completed his project," and he concluded the dictation.

We all dashed out—Mark and Elizabeth too—and Morya was gone. But there was a little garden shed out in the back where we kept our tools, and the radiation there was so strong it nearly knocked us over. That is where Morya had set his electrode, anchored his vibration. He wanted us to turn that tiny little shed into our private prayer chapel, our Will of God focus. This is probably as close as we will ever come to being physically in El Morya's presence. He was actually walking our property to raise the vibration of the area.

The First Conference at the Motherhouse, Easter 1970

After about a year of remodeling, the Motherhouse was ready for our first guests. Mark and several staff drove out in his gold bus about three or four days before the Easter conference 1970. Elizabeth remained home working on the book and flew out just before the conference opened.

The Motherhouse in Santa Barbara

In the front of this previous Jewish synagogue was a large semi-circular driveway, and between it and the street was a huge cactus garden. Century plants and other large cacti had been growing there for years. Mark said, "Look at that cactus garden. It's not a lawn!" I answered, "Well, when you bought it, that was the way it was."

Mark replied, "Look at that cactus over there, Mrs. Booth. It is called a 'crown of thorns.' Those were the thorns that pricked Jesus' brow when they crucified him. I refuse to have that in my Motherhouse. I will not give my first dictation in Santa Barbara with these things on my property."

So we spent all the next day with ropes tied to our cars, pulling out these huge century plants, as tall as a man and six feet across. I had planned on spending those few days preparing for the conference instead of pulling out cacti.

With relief I said, "Okay, Mark, they're out. Now what?" He answered, "Well, put in a lawn, of course." I moaned, "Mark, the conference starts tomorrow." He said, "That's alright. I just read an advertisement where nurseries have sod. You can just roll out a beautiful lawn in front of my

Motherhouse. Now, get busy! The conference starts tomorrow, and I want things to look nice." And so, the day before the Easter conference we were out in front rolling out a new lawn. I soon realized that Mark and Elizabeth were not living in the realm of time and space. They could give the most amazing assignments, absolutely impossible, and yet expect them to be completed in about one-tenth of the time necessary. And, you know, somehow we were able to do it!

By now I thought things were going rather smoothly until Mark said, "By the way, Mrs. Booth, I've been walking around and looking over things and I noticed that you didn't make any curtains for those two little back windows over there." I had not had time and thought it really wasn't necessary anyway. He said, "Okay, I want curtains right away, today, throughout the entire house or I don't want any conference." And so, of course, I went downtown and bought more material and made curtains immediately.

A couple of weeks earlier I had just survived the "curtain crisis" in our reading room. We had windows covering one entire wall on the front of the house, facing the street. Anita Buchanan, who was an excellent seamstress, had come out from La Tourelle especially for the purpose of making those curtains. We went down to the salesroom in Los Angeles and purchased soft blue chiffon to make a criss-cross arrangement covering the entire wall. I bought several bolts of material to make a lovely full drape for this twenty-foot-wide window from ceiling to floor. (In fact, I bought all of the material this particular salesroom had in stock.)

Several days later I came in to admire the finished effect when I saw to my horror that one of the panels was about eighteen inches shorter than the others. Anita said, "I must have measured wrong. You will have to buy me more material." When I told her that there was no more material available, she said, "Just leave me alone and let me think."

About an hour later I returned to see a beautiful sweep of

blue chiffon curtains, absolutely etheric and all the same length, just barely touching the floor. I said, "Anita, what did you do?" She said, "I just said, 'Saint Germain, I am in serious trouble. You just have to do something!' And he stretched it."

I refused to allow these curtains to be washed for several years, afraid that Saint Germain's "stretching" might shrink again when I put it in the wash. However, nothing happened. His miracle was permanent.

I really didn't think anything else could possibly happen until Mark called me into the sanctuary. He said, "Mrs. Booth, this color on the wall of the sanctuary is not pink enough." And I said, "Mark, I sent you a sample of the paint and you okayed it." He said, "I can't help it. It is not pink enough. Now, stand here with me, and I must make this a deeper shade of pink." And as a result of his prayers and chants, one could just see the pink paint slowly grow pinker! (If there is such a word.)

One last thing that I remember about our Easter conference was that on the morning when it opened, the men were still laying pink carpet on the podium. The class was to start at 2:00 p.m. and the men were still laying carpet at 1:30. We almost had heart failure because people were arriving from all over the world. However, all's well that ends well!

We had a beautiful Easter conference, and then the day after the conference we all took off for a three-week tour of India. That is when I realized what the human body can endure and still stay alive.

CHAPTER EIGHT

INDIA

AFTER REMODELING the Motherhouse and holding our Easter conference, the Class of the Resurrection Flame, seventy of us took off the next morning from Santa Barbara on a pilgrimage to India—March 30, 1970. Visiting India had always been a special dream of mine. And here we were, actually on our way! We left Santa Barbara directly for India via New York and Amsterdam.

Bombay

I remember my first glimpse of a tall Indian in a turban. It was in the airport, immediately after we disembarked from our plane in Bombay. The moment I saw that turban, I knew I was really home! Past life memories of Indian embodiments flooded through my mind and made the heat, noises, smells and chaos of India almost familiar to me.

It took a bit of getting used to the traffic—tiny taxis weaving in and out at breakneck speed with little regard for life and limb; elephants, cows, camels walking serenely down the middle of the street, entirely oblivious of the cars; crowds of people on bicycles and rickshaws; and even pedestrians constantly crossing the streets wherever they pleased. There were traffic policemen standing on little boxes at the intersections, wearing white gloves and endeavoring to direct traffic. But no one, except us, really paid any attention to them.

Dressing in the Color of the Day

We had been given instruction by the ascended masters that on each day of the week there is released from the heart of the sun a special concentration of one of the seven rainbow rays of God. Yellow, the color of illumination, is sent to earth on Sunday, the day of the sun. Pink, the symbol of divine love, is released on Monday. Tuesday's color is blue, the symbol of faith, power and the will of God. Green, the blending of blue and yellow, is the color of truth and healing. This ray is released on Wednesday. Purple and gold with ruby flecks, the ray of ministration and service, is Thursday's ray. Friday is the day of purity and the ascension, the white ray. And Saturday is our violet day, blending the rays of love and power, the pink and the blue, from which we receive the violet flame of freedom, mercy and transmutation.

Since the purpose of our pilgrimage was to return the light of the West back to the East again, we chose the date immediately following the Easter class when we would all be filled with the light of the resurrection flame. In fact, all those who were to be pilgrims to India spent six weeks prior to Easter Sunday giving prayers and mantras to the flame of the resurrection.

And so, we decided to all dress in the color of the ray of the day in order to spread more radiation wherever we traveled. Women were asked to bring seven lightweight dresses in the colors of the seven rays. Men wore bow ties in the appropriate color of the day. I can tell you, we made quite an impact wherever we went! Seventy individuals all wearing the same color at the same time. We were stopped everywhere we went by people wanting to know what this meant. It gave us an excellent opportunity to open a conversation on the teachings of the ascended masters.

We traveled throughout India on tour buses, rather primitive ones compared to those in the United States, accompanied by a guide who explained the history of the country through which we were passing. We spent much of the time singing one of our violet flame songs to the melody of Santa Lucia. Our driver and guide soon learned the words and were singing happily with us. When the bus stopped for a moment, crowds of Indians would gather to enjoy our singing and often joined in. We found throughout India very devotional people responsive to the flame we were bearing.

I AM the Violet Flame

I AM the violet flame
In action in me now
I AM the violet flame
To light alone I bow
I AM the violet flame
In mighty cosmic power
I AM the light of God
Shining every hour
I AM the violet flame
Blazing like a sun
I AM God's sacred power
Freeing every one.

The Dalai Lama

One of the highlights of our tour was a trip to Dharmsala to visit the Dalai Lama in exile. This is the home they have built in India since they were forced to flee persecutions in Tibet. I couldn't help but contrast the starkness of these cement-block buildings with the beauty and wealth of the golden Potala, the Dalai Lama's former residence in Tibet.

We rode for about six hours in a tiny little bus, up curvy mountain roads to Dharmsala. In fact, the space between the seats was so small that I remember seeing Mark, who was six feet, two inches tall, lying on the floor in the aisle at one time to ease his aching back.

There was a religious observance taking place on the day of our visit. Pilgrims had been arriving from all over India and Tibet, many on foot. There were bright prayer flags strung up on the trees for miles to welcome these travelers. We were fortunate to be granted an audience by the Dalai Lama, and Mark and

After an 8-hour bus ride to Dharmsala high in the Himalayan Mountains near Kashmir, the Prophets and their tour were received by the Dalai Lama in his private quarters and by Secretary, Tenzin Geyche, who also acted as his interpreter. His Holiness is joking about Sean Prophet's Tibetan hat.

Elizabeth talked to him for about a half hour concerning the teachings of the ascended masters. I was impressed by his humility. He shook hands with each one of us personally as we left.

We were allowed into their temple where Mark joined the monks in chanting Buddhist mantras. They have an exquisite golden Buddha about ten feet high. I have no idea how such a large and valuable statue was ever brought all those miles from Tibet and across those rugged mountains. Whenever I hear on the news today about the persecutions of the Tibetan people, I remember our trip to the Dalai Lama and his devotees in Dharmsala, India. And my heart goes out to them in their affliction.

Mother Teresa

We were privileged to meet in person not only the Dalai Lama but also Mother Teresa of Calcutta. This blessed modern-day saint was an inspiration to all of us. You could feel the love radiating from this tiny little person dressed in her white cotton sari with the blue border.

As busy as she was, she still spent several hours with us and showed us around her ashram. One vignette I especially remember is seeing her nuns out in the open courtyard, doing their mountain of laundry by hand with only a bucket of water and soap for each one. That was in 1970, and the situation may have changed now since Mother Teresa and her work have become well known. But at the time of our visit there were few conveniences at hand.

We were struck by the love, joy and peace radiating from all the nuns and the entire ashram in the midst of all their busy, physical activities. She showed us their prayer chapel and reminded us that they could not possibly endure the life they were living and their service to the "poorest of the poor" if they did not have a personal life of devotion and dedication to Jesus and his mission.

Mark and Elizabeth meeting with Mother Teresa

There is no need for me to describe Mother Teresa's life and service, not only in Calcutta but also internationally, as her service expanded and she became a well-known figure throughout the world. Many excellent books tell us about her life's work. Her recent death was felt by all races and religions, and her funeral has been televised for all to see. I felt privileged to have had the opportunity to meet this blessed soul in person.

The River Ganges

Our boat ride on the Ganges was a memorable occasion. We were riding in an open boat and Elizabeth, the children and many of our group kept diving overboard for a quick swim as we floated down the river. We were able to witness a cremation at one of the burning ghats on the shore.

The Ganges is a focal point of life for many Indians. We saw women using the river to do their laundry and then spreading the wet clothes along the banks to dry in the sun. I could not understand why the clothes didn't become muddy, but all of them were snowy white. Although the waters looked muddy and thousands used the Ganges for daily bathing, scientific tests have shown that the water is pure. Millions of devotees revere their "Mother Ganges" as a holy river.

At one place our boat landed and we walked up hundreds of steps to a monastery. Mark Prophet was accepted wherever we went, as Indians recognized his attainment. Indian yogis seemed to be more perceptive than Americans. On his visit to Rishikesh, the abbot invited Mark to sit with him and meditate in his ashram. We learned several Indian chants and mantras from the monks at the various ashrams we visited throughout India.

Darjeeling

Naturally, we could not leave India without visiting Darjeeling, the retreat of the Ascended Master El Morya. His retreat is in the etheric octave over the physical city of Darjeeling, and yet you can feel his presence throughout the entire area.

Mark meeting a holy man of India

Darjeeling is a city in Northeast India in West Bengal on the border of Sikkim, high in the Himalayas. Our bus could only take us so far, and then we had to continue to climb either by a tiny little train, a little narrow-gauge railroad that winds its way up and up and up, or by tiny taxis. Mark decided that the best choice for the seventy pilgrims in our group would be taxis.

Mark always liked to drive and, in fact, preferred to do the driving himself because he didn't care to have anyone else accountable for his life. He surveyed these little taxis and the winding, steep, narrow road and said, "Mrs. Booth, I have two choices. One is to tell this man, who doesn't speak English, that I want to drive his car. I am certain that he will say 'No.' The second is to sit here and go into samadhi.* So, you are going to sit beside me and don't touch me. But the moment we get to Darjeeling you wake me up. I am not going to watch this road."

So Mark went into samadhi, and we endured those miles

and miles of curves. He was so close to heaven that he could slip into deep meditation in a moment. Heaven was just natural to him. But for the rest of us, it took three and one half uncomfortable hours by motor car from Bhagdogra to Darjeeling—a trip of only fifty miles. El Morya once remarked on Mark's mercurial ability to go to the heights of samadhi instantly. He said Mark was just like an express elevator going up and coming back to earth.

The trip would have been interesting if we had not kept our eyes glued to that curvy road. We passed the terraced hills where Darjeeling tea is grown on the mountainside. Every so often we passed through small Tibetan villages and all the children came out to stare at us and wave as we drove along.

Eventually we arrived in Darjeeling and saw the tall pines that Morya speaks of in his dictations. The scent of pine permeated the entire area. Darjeeling is an interesting town, perched almost on the top of the world in the Himalayas. It is a no-nonsense town, just as you would expect a one-pointed master like Morya to be.

You could feel the pulsations of the will of God and Morya's radiance from his etheric Retreat of the Will of God above Darjeeling.

We stayed at the Oberoi Grand Hotel in Darjeeling, plagued by constant power outages and plumbing difficulties. The weather was very cold in April at this rim of the world and many of us had not brought along warm enough clothing for this high altitude.

Sunrise Over Mount Kanchenjunga

Another of the sights we were determined to see in India was Mount Kanchenjunga, the mountain printed on the masthead of several Summit publications. Our tour guide assured us that there would be no problem.

And so, we left our hotel at 4:00 a.m. on a bitterly cold morning and drove up in the Himalayas to see the sun rise. Our destination was Tiger Hill, about seven miles from Darjeeling. Mark was the wisest one of us all—he took his blanket from the hotel with him. I can see him yet, standing there in the dim light leading us in singing "How Great Thou Art." Here he was, with his blanket wrapped around him and wearing that fur hat that made him look so Russian. And there we stood, shivering and feeling as though we would soon be frozen statues! And we sang, and we sang, and we sang—all of Mark's favorite songs, "Jesus of Galilee," "The Holy City," and many others.

About 7:00 a.m. we were still singing and decreeing. Finally Mark asked the tour guide, "What time is the sun supposed to come up?" We had not yet caught a glimpse of Kanchenjunga. The mountain was still completely shrouded in fog and clouds. The guide answered, "Oh, the sun does not come up this time of year. There are only about three weeks during the entire year when you can catch a glimpse of Kanchenjunga."

We learned that Indians like to please and will tell you whatever they think you want to hear. That is why he was willing to conduct us up the mountain to see the sunrise even though he knew perfectly well it was impossible this time of year.

But today, anytime I sing "How Great Thou Art," in my mind's eye I can still see us standing high up in the Himalayas, shivering and waiting for the sun to come up over Mount Kanchenjunga. I can still hear Mark's beautiful voice leading us in song.

On our way back down to Darjeeling, we stopped for a few hours at Ghoom Monastery. Mark and some of the men blew those six-foot long horns that we have often seen on television lately in the documentaries on Tibet.

Srinagar

We couldn't leave India without visiting Srinagar, where Kuthumi's retreat is located in the etheric plane. Srinagar is just

Mark on Dal Lake, Kashmir

as different from Darjeeling as Kuthumi is different from El Morya. It is one of the most beautiful spots I have ever seen on earth! We arrived when it was spring and the lilacs were blooming in profusion. Their fragrance and the radiation over the entire area of Dal Lake was almost overpowering. In fact, the entire group of seventy pilgrims decided to lie on the ground and just bask in the radiance of Kuthumi's retreat. This was the place where Kuthumi was born in one of his embodiments, and we could still feel the strong radiation in this physical area.

We went out on Dal Lake, and immediately swarms of small boats came out from every direction trying to sell us their wares. And let me tell you, there are excellent salesmen in India! Many of us went home with trinkets that we really did not know why we purchased except that it seemed the right thing to do at the moment.

It saddens me today to hear of the conflict of Moslem Pakistan and Hindu India over the ownership of Kashmir, located between the two nations. I could go on and on about India and our experiences on that trip, but the India tour is only one of my many memories of Mark.

CHAPTER NINE

MEMORIES OF THE MOTHERHOUSE

UP UNTIL THIS POINT I have endeavored to present my memories in a fairly correct chronological sequence. Now, however, I must depart from any semblance of order, since the anecdotes I am about to relate about life at the Motherhouse in Santa Barbara were so interwoven with what transpired at La Tourelle that it is impossible to narrate them sequentially.

During all the time we were remodeling the Motherhouse and, in fact, during all the years until Mark's ascension in 1973, I kept flying back and forth between Santa Barbara and Colorado Springs. I really had two homes and two different sets of assignments and duties during these years.

I was actively participating in the final editing and preparation of *Climb the Highest Mountain* for publication in Colorado Springs at the same time as I was the director, or "housemother," of the Motherhouse in Santa Barbara. I became quite a frequent flyer in the days before the airlines announced their free-ticket plan.

Painting the Lawn Green

At one time Mark came to Santa Barbara for a Christmas conference. He was not accustomed to life in California since he had lived his entire life in the East and Midwest. He was appalled to see that the large lawn in back in the formal garden had turned brown and appeared dead. He expected everything to be perpetually green in California.

He took one look and said, "Mrs. Booth, why did you let my lawn die?" I said, "Mark this lawn isn't dead. This is lipia grass, a very sturdy form of lawn universally used in Santa Barbara. December and January are the dormant times. It will be fine again in a couple of months."

His answer to me was, "Well, I refuse to have a Christmas conference with dead grass. What are you going to do about it?" My flippant reply was, "Well, I don't know, unless you want me to paint it green." I wished that I had bit my tongue when he said, "Yes, Mrs. Booth, that is exactly what I want you to do—paint my lawn green."

Mark had seen an advertisement the previous day for a type of spray paint for lawns. He said, "Get some of your men, buy some green paint, get spray guns and paint my lawn green. Hurry, you only have two days before the conference and it will need time to dry before people can sit on it."

I was very embarrassed when I went to the nursery and said, "Pardon me, but do you happen to have any green paint for brown lawns?" The salesman was delighted to find someone who wanted to buy this new product.

An entire crew of men went to work with their little spray guns and "painted the lawn green." It was quite an undertaking, because we had a very large expanse of lawn in the formal garden at the rear of the Motherhouse. But the next day we had the most beautiful green lawn you could ever ask for so that Mark could open his Christmas conference—in fact, the *only* green lawn in Santa Barbara.

Living with Mark Prophet was certainly an education. He had absolutely no sense of limitation and accepted nothing as impossible. Almost every assignment he gave me seemed impossible, and yet somehow it was finished satisfactorily and on time. I learned so much from him and am so grateful for having been granted these years with him.

Saint Bonaventure

One day we walked over to the Santa Barbara Mission, just about two blocks from the Motherhouse. There was a large tapestry, probably twelve feet tall, of Saint Bonaventure in the foyer as we entered. As we were admiring it, El Morya spoke to Mark and said, "Mark, that is you!"

Mark was very humble when he realized that this had been one of his embodiments. The story is told that his mother brought her child who was ill, almost at the point of death, to Saint Francis. Francis prayed and the little boy was healed. Those who witnessed this miracle exclaimed, "Oh, Bonaventura!" (good fortune) and rejoiced. His mother consecrated her son to a life of service to God and he was thereafter called Bonaventure.

As he grew older he became a member of Saint Francis' monks, the Franciscans, and was one of the leaders in that order after Francis' death. Bonaventure became one of the saints of the Catholic Church and later one of the doctors of the Church—the Seraphic Doctor, as he was called—as he endeavored to set forth the true doctrines.

A Lesson in Administration

Mark and Elizabeth and their family, together with a few staff members, were accustomed to riding out to Santa Barbara several times a year for quarterly conferences. At the time this incident occurred, one of the children was still in diapers. In those days, diaper services and disposable diapers were not commonly in vogue. The acceptable method was to take a dirty diaper and rinse it in the toilet.

Well, this particular evening the caretaker lost her hold on the diaper and it was flushed down the toilet. We had had a difficult time with our plumbing anyway since the house was perhaps fifty years old and the clay drainage tiles were wearing out. Santa Barbara is in the semitropical zone and roots have a tendency to grow in between the tiles and impede the drainage. We were in the habit of calling the Roto Rooter man regularly.

I realized immediately that I was in trouble. The conference was starting the next day and Mark was asleep in his gold bus in the driveway. The maintenance man came out, dug a deep hole and a long trench and turned on floodlights that lighted up the entire area. And still Mark slept (or so I thought) amid all the noise of the Roto Rooter and the bright lights. I thought, "Well, I'm certainly getting out of this one easy."

The next morning, before the conference, Mark took me aside and said, "Mrs. Booth, what was the problem last night?" I answered, "No problem, Mark, that I know of." He said, "Well, I heard some noises." I said, "Oh that was just the Roto Rooter man. We have problems with our plumbing periodically. Everything is fine now." Mark said, "What happened, Mrs. Booth?" I said, "Well, it doesn't matter. It is all fixed now."

He continued, "Are you going to tell me what happened?" I said, "Well, I guess a diaper was flushed down the toilet." And he said, "Oh, and who did it?" And I said, "It really doesn't matter, Mark. It is all taken care of." He said, "You have been in The Summit Lighthouse long enough to know that I know who did it. And I am telling you right now that you are never going to protect anyone from me. Now, *who did it?*"

And so, of course, I had to tell him. As a result I proceeded to get at least a half-hour lecture from Mark Prophet, while the caregiver who precipitated the crisis never heard a word about it from him.

I learned the hard way that as long as I was in charge of the focus, Mark trusted me implicitly. But in order for him to have that trust, he needed to know that I was completely honest with him. I was given a lot of freedom in my choices and actions but, in return, I also had a lot of responsibility—not the least of which was to accurately report events at the Motherhouse in a timely fashion to Mark Prophet.

"Trust No Man!"

I couldn't tell you how often I have heard Mark admonish me, "Trust no man!"* No matter how hard I tried, I always

---

*These words are a direct quotation. However, in no way are they intended to be a statement of gender. The meaning is, "Trust no one. Trust only the Divine and not the human."

seemed naïve in certain situations. I have an innate trust of people that sometimes works to my detriment. The first time I was taken in by a story that seemed plausible but later proved to be a fabrication to get a staff member out of trouble, Mark took me aside and proceeded to enlighten me.

He said that El Morya had a serious message for me. It was, "Trust no man! Trust only God." Mark said that I had a direct tie to my Christ Self and God Presence if I would only trust my intuition. He said that if I would trust only God and not man, I would have fewer problems in my administrative duties. I tried to remember this but would occasionally drop back into the habit of accepting peoples' rationalizations. And then in my mind I could hear Mark's words, "Mrs. Booth, remember: 'Trust no man!'"

Snack Bar

The Motherhouse is about a mile from the center of Santa Barbara, and when people went downtown for lunch during conferences, they often became sidetracked by the lovely beach area and arrived late and missed part of the first afternoon event. I thought I would try an innovation to solve this problem.

I started a snack bar consisting of very simple food, served buffet style on the large lawn in the formal garden in back. (Always green both summer and winter!) The menu consisted mainly of brown rice, soup, sandwiches, apple juice and herb tea. I remember carrying hundreds of gallons of apple juice in my little Mustang convertible to sell by the glass at lunchtime and at breaks.

The snack bar became a popular addition to our Santa Barbara conferences. The weather was always warm, and those attending enjoyed the opportunity to relax on the lawn and talk with their friends. Another item in our favor was that Mark was constantly available for informal chats with the students. No one seemed to mind the fact that the menu was always the same. The fellowship, and especially an opportunity to talk

Mark taking advantage of the snack bar at the Motherhouse

with Mark personally, became more important than a variety of foods. The snack bar was so popular that we eventually adopted the idea of a snack bar for use at classes at La Tourelle.

The Ascended Master University at the Motherhouse

On the morning after the Freedom Conference, Monday, July 5, 1971, Mark Prophet inaugurated AMU, the Ascended Master University on the Santa Barbara campus. This first session was a two-week seminar attended by young and old alike. The students who attended were from all walks of life—

those interested in furthering their own spiritual experiences and also those who were interested in teaching or conducting student study groups in their hometowns. There were classes in Comparative World Religions, the Historical Design of the Bible, The Brotherhood and God-Government and Mark's own daily class on Cosmic Law. There was an emphasis on physical rejuvenation—classes on vegetarian cooking, diet for the expectant mother and children, fasting, reflexology, herbs, gardening and all that is required for the spiritual man and woman to live a successful and fulfilling life.

AMU was to give a sense of purpose in life, to teach how God's mercy works through cosmic law, and to present to students an opportunity to surrender undesirable habit patterns and momentums of which they really wanted to rid themselves.

The reason for the emphasis on the elements of diet and physical rejuvenation was that in the early 1970s many young souls were becoming enmeshed in the psychedelic drug culture. Many of these were sincere seekers trying to find the meaning of life, and yet they had wandered unknowingly into the bypass of the world of drugs.

AMU was striving to teach that psychedelic drugs and the complexities of life are not the answer—that life can be lived gloriously and beautifully through the awareness of the teachings of the ascended masters. Mark was present every day, not only teaching but also offering himself as a counselor and friend to these young people.

Mark's original plan was to implement the ascended masters' dream of a school where people of all ages can be taught the synthesis between the spiritual and the physical branches of ascended master and human knowledge.

His faith and vision extended beyond this first session. He predicted that the masters' university would eventually be on every continent and in every country throughout the world. Mark made a treasure map for the organization years ago, a mental map. He put down all his projected plans, subject to

God's will. And many of them have already come to pass. He envisioned the thousands of members that we have in the organization today.

Attendance at AMU, the Ascended Masters' University program, offered the opportunity of the centuries whereby the heavenly host make available to mankind at large in the physical octave the courses of instruction that are taught in the etheric retreats of the masters.

I would like to quote from Mark's original brochure telling about AMU. I think it best explains his dream:

"Have you longed to see a school where religion and science meet, where you can learn practical ideas that will enable you to understand life and its mysteries and to help others do likewise?

"Have you been looking for a way to qualify yourself to properly present spiritual truth to a seeking humanity in this stage of world struggle?

"Here is your opportunity to gain a practical understanding of how to utilize your energies and talents in the ascended master way in order that you may qualify as an adept of ascended master law and new age teacher. Now is the time for you to master these fundamentals."

And then, after Mark's ascension, under the direction of Elizabeth Clare Prophet, we expanded AMU to become a twelve-week session four times a year. We eventually changed its name to Summit University as we continued holding classes in Pasadena, at Camelot in Los Angeles, and later at the Royal Teton Ranch in Montana. With the addition of our school of theology and training for the ordination of ministers, our eventual goal is a four-year fully accredited university.

CHAPTER TEN

THE HOLY LAND

AFTER OUR MEMORABLE TRIP to India, we were all eager to accompany Mark again when he suggested a pilgrimage to the Holy Land. The plan was for the tour to depart in September of 1972.

Final chapters of *Climb the Highest Mountain* had just been printed and sent off to the bindery. The writing and editing of this book had consumed much of the messengers' time for several years. Mark thought that now was the perfect time to realize his dream of visiting the Holy Land.

I knew that I also wanted to see the Holy Land—more than any other spot on earth. In my days as a child, when I was a fundamentalist Baptist, I used to pore through the pictures in my Bible and dream of the day when I could visit the lands where Abraham, Moses, Jesus and the apostles had walked.

Although money had never been a particular problem in my life, at this moment my husband and I did not have the necessary amount of cash for this trip. (It was before the days of the widespread use of credit cards.) I had been in charge of selling the tickets for our India tour whereby the travel agent gave one free tour for each seven tickets sold. That is how we were able to go to India.

Now, I knew that it would not be fair for us to receive the free tickets a second time. There were so many other staff who had had to stay home from India and who wanted to go to the Holy Land.

Before we came on staff, my husband and I had accumulated a goodly store of antiques. We had supported ourselves for the last several years by selling them off one by one. This had been our reason for collecting these antiques—to support ourselves in our retirement.

And so, we really weren't worried about where our funds would come from for our trip to the Holy Land. My husband had recently restored a Ford Model A car. He said, "Well, here is my ticket to the Holy Land. I know I can sell it for at least $1,500." And I replied, "Fine, and I will just sell one of my antique clocks." I knew that they were absolutely beautiful and were worth much more than the ticket price.

Well, his car sold immediately and he had the money for his ticket right away. But my grandfather clock didn't sell. And it did not sell. And it did not sell. I knew I couldn't ask Mark for a free ticket this time because he wouldn't give it to me since he had already invited other staff members to accompany him.

I had been working with Mark at La Tourelle as his correspondence secretary. (More about this later.) Just about a week before our tour was to depart, he said, "You had better go home to Santa Barbara now, get your things in order and get ready to go with us." I had completed every possible detail in his office in preparation for this trip, and so there was really no more work for me in Colorado Springs.

My Test of Obedience

No sooner had I returned to Santa Barbara than I received a phone call from Mark the next morning. "Mrs. Booth, I want you to come back here on the noon plane." I was amazed. My reply was, "Mark, I was just there yesterday. I cleaned up everything in your office. There is no more work to be done, and if I don't stay here, my clock won't sell. And then I can't go to the Holy Land."

I had gone on a whirlwind of cleaning and had pulled everything out in the driveway. Mark said, "Let someone else put it back in place. You be on that 1:00 p.m. plane!" I don't know if you have ever tried to argue with Mark Prophet. You can do it just so long, and then you realize the futility of it all.

I decided to give it one more try—the final argument for my remaining in Santa Barbara. I said again, "Mark, my clock hasn't sold, and if I don't stay here and sell it, I can't go to the Holy Land with you." His answer was, "Well, that's the way it is. Be on that plane!"

When that line of reasoning didn't work, I made one last futile attempt. I said, "Mark, every other time I've come to you, I've paid my own airfare. I don't have any money now." (Again, this was before the days of credit cards.) He answered, "I'll pay your airline ticket to come back to La Tourelle. Now, get on that plane, Mrs. Booth!"

When I realized that I couldn't oppose him any longer, I asked meekly, "Could I please come on the six o'clock plane tonight instead of noon?" He answered, "Alright, but be sure you don't miss the plane."

And so that evening I walked in the back door of La Tourelle, where I had just left the day before with my suitcase. Everyone who saw me said, "Oh, what are you back here again for?" All I could say was, "I don't have any idea why I am back, but here I am." Mark wasn't even home. When I looked in his office, I was right: there wasn't a bit of work awaiting me. I went straight down to my room and went to sleep.

I spent the next three days at La Tourelle and did not do a lick of work because there was no work to do. In fact, I did not even see Mark all this time. You can imagine by now that my state of consciousness was pretty horrible. Everyone kept saying, "Annice, this is the silliest thing I have ever heard. What are you here for anyway? Why aren't you in Santa Barbara getting ready to leave for the Holy Land?" Of course, I was also asking myself the same questions. We were supposed to depart in only five days.

I finally saw Mark on about the third day I was there. He just said, "Hello, Mrs. Booth." And walked right on.

A little later, I received a phone call from Santa Barbara from a sweet little Chinese lady. She said, "Annice, your clock hasn't sold." My rather sarcastic reply was, "Well, what else is new? I'm not going to the Holy Land."

She answered, "Oh, no, dear. I'm ninety years old and too old to go. I fell asleep when we visited the Dalai Lama on our India tour. I am going to give you my ticket." I objected two or three times just to be polite and then said, "I'll take it! I'll take it! I'll take it!"

Mark saw me sitting there in absolute shock and said, "What are you sitting there for? Why aren't you working?" I answered, "Well, in the first place, there is no work to do and you know that. In the second place, I'm going to the Holy Land!" He simply replied, "Well, of course you are. I thought you knew it all along."

Then he proceeded to buzz five times to call everyone together for a staff meeting. You could be sure that when you heard those five buzzes, it meant that everyone was to drop whatever work they were doing and congregate immediately in the sanctuary—oftentimes to hear what Mrs. Booth had done now.

This time, if you can believe it, he wanted to tell everyone about Mrs. Booth's *obedience.* He said that El Morya had told him to make sure that I returned to La Tourelle the next day and Mark did not dare tell me why. He said that I was arguing so much with him that he was really afraid that I wouldn't come. Mark wanted me to go to the Holy Land, but he knew perfectly well that El Morya would not allow me to go if I did not pass the test of obedience by returning to La Tourelle.

By that time the whole intensity of the situation started to dawn on me. I raised my hand in the staff meeting and said, "Mark, are you telling me that if I hadn't come out here when you called, that I would not have been allowed to go the Holy Land?" He said, "Absolutely, Mrs. Booth. And I was so afraid I was going to lose you, the way you were arguing. I wanted you to come with us, but I was really scared that you were failing a test of obedience."

As I was sitting there contemplating the gravity of the situation and how nearly I had come to losing one of my life's dreams, Mark said, "Mrs. Booth, what are you sitting here for? Go home and pack so that you can go to the Holy Land with us."

(Just as an aside—my clock never did sell. And so I gave it to the messenger for the Santa Barbara focus.)

The reason I am telling you this is that you may not realize a direct test coming from the master any more than I did. This time Mark did not dare to intervene and wasn't allowed to tell me why I should return immediately to La Tourelle. In fact, there was nothing more ridiculous than my coming back out there so soon—moneywise and for every other reason.

We are closer to heaven and the ascended masters' path of initiation than we realize. We may be walking a slippery path if we try to rely only on our own human reasoning and common sense.

My test was one of absolute obedience, even though I "knew not the reason why." Yours may come in a completely different way. You may only find the reason, as I did, after you have obeyed. If you do not follow when your Christ Self speaks to you, you may fail an important initiation and lose a major blessing that the masters wish to bestow upon you.

Cairo

And so, on September 18, 1972, our group of pilgrims took off on our flight for the Holy Land. The first stopover was Athens, Greece, and then we were on our way to Egypt.

In Cairo we visited the church where Mother Mary appeared to the faithful. Photographers have taken a picture of her in her light body hovering over the dome of this Coptic Church. Although she had appeared several years previously, there was still a large crowd of devotees praying at this church when we were there. We could still feel Mother Mary's radiation.

Cairo's Egyptian museum is one of the most renowned in the world. We searched through the collection of mummies trying to find the one of Ikhnaton (Amenhotep IV), pharaoh of

Mark and Elizabeth on camels, Holy Land tour.

Egypt 1353–1336 B.C. This was one of Mark Prophet's earlier embodiments when, as pharaoh, he departed from the old religion of many gods and established the worship of Aton, the One God. Aton was depicted as the sun disk. Ikhnaton drew the rays coming from the sun and ending in hands extending out in all directions. This signified that there is only one God but many manifestations in form. We are extensions of that One.

We were riding along in our tour bus just a few feet beyond the suburb of the modern city of Cairo, when suddenly right in front of us rose the Sphinx and the Great Pyramid of Giza. We were amazed at the immediate transformation from houses and cultivated fields to complete desert and the pyramids. And then, of course, we each had to have a ride on a camel, as tourists do, so that we could send a photograph back home.

The merchants of Cairo are persistent and often unscrupulous, as we found to our sorrow. As we wandered among the narrow streets and bazaars in the old section of the city, our guide recommended one certain perfume merchant to us for his excellent prices and the good quality of his merchandise. We selected several large bottles of various fragrances to take home. We planned to put them into smaller bottles to sell to our Keepers of the Flame* at our next conference as mementos of our Holy Land trip. We spent quite a length of time inspecting the various scents and finally placed a rather large order, certain that we could recoup our money quickly when we returned home.

Imagine our surprise and dismay when we returned home to find that all the bottles were filled with *water!* I suspect that our Egyptian tour guide probably received a certain percentage from the merchant for steering us to his shop. Oh well, live and learn!

Luxor

One of the highlights of our tour was to have been a visit to Luxor and the etheric location of Serapis Bey's Ascension Temple. As we were in the airport at Cairo awaiting our flight, the news came over the loudspeaker that our flight had been cancelled. Fighting had accelerated between the Israelis and Arabs and the airline refused to take responsibility for our safety.

This trip to Luxor and the possibility of a dictation by Serapis Bey were planned as one of the main highlights of the trip. While we all prayed and prayed in the airport and Mark tried to negotiate with the officials, the answer was an unequivocal, "No, you may not travel to Luxor any time in the near future by plane, by bus or by any carrier."

We returned to our hotel, a rather dispirited group of devotees. The only place we could assemble was in the restaurant. And that night in our hotel in Cairo Serapis Bey dictated. In fact, if you listen to the tape of the dictation, you can hear the dishes clinking in the background in the kitchen as they were being washed. Serapis said, "Dear hearts, you really did not think you had to come to Luxor personally to find me, did you?" We realized then how silly our worries had been.

Saladin

One of Mark's embodiments was Saladin, the great Moslem sultan of Egypt and Syria. During one of the Crusades, he fought Richard the Lionhearted of England for the possession of Jerusalem. History records the benevolence of Saladin in his battles as opposed to the cruelty and bloodthirstiness of the Christians in their attempt to conquer Jerusalem from the infidels, as they called the Moslems of Saladin's troops. When Saladin captured Jerusalem, he extended mercy to the people—Arabs and Christians alike.

We stood at Saladin's tomb at Damascus and photographed his portrait. We brought this photograph home as a momento for Mark's office.

The memory of this embodiment was still vivid in Mark's mind as we visited the Dome of the Rock, a spiritual focus for the Moslem world. This mosque was built on the spot where Solomon's Temple stood before the Romans destroyed it. We all gathered round to offer chants and prayers and sound the OM but were quickly ushered unceremoniously out of the temple. Apparently it is only a focus for the worship of Islam today.

The Dead Sea Scrolls and Megiddo

It was a thrill to actually see the original Dead Sea Scrolls in their museum, the Palestine Archaeological Museum (now called the Rockefeller Museum), located in the Arabic Eastern quarter of the city of Jerusalem. This exhibit brought back to many of us memories of our lives in the Essene Community from about 100 B.C. to A.D 68.

Many of the scrolls that were found hidden in jars in caves near Qumran are torn and damaged in spots, but many are still in a remarkable state of preservation. The actual building that houses the scrolls is a beautiful example of modern-day architecture in the midst of these barren desert hills.

Before we left the area, we wanted to visit the Dead Sea, a lake several hundred feet below sea level, and dip our toes in the warm salt water.

Reading Climb the Highest Mountain *in the Holy Land*

I can still see Mark and Elizabeth sitting on the hill of Megiddo, which was an ancient city in Palestine, north of Samaria. *Climb the Highest Mountain* had just been bound and a copy had been air freighted to them on their Holy Land tour. Mark was reading to us from the book. He said that if the battle of Armegeddon ever densified into the physical, it would be fought beneath us here on the plains of Armageddon, beneath the hill of Megiddo.

We visited Beirut, a modern city in Lebanon, and also Baalbek. These ruins remind us of the times when human sacrifice, as a part of religious offerings to the god Baal, was practiced in the area.

And now, on to the old city of Jerusalem to visit the locations made memorable by Jesus' life and mission.

Jerusalem

When we arrived in Jerusalem we found, in reality, two cities—one of the most modern on the planet and also the old city, replete with history and memories.

Jerusalem is a city revered as holy by Christians, Jews and Moslems alike. These three sects all claim the patriarch Abraham as their father and founder. Much friction and even warfare has arisen over the years as a result, because each group claims the holy places as their own.

I can remember walking the stations of the cross in those dark, narrow streets of Old Jerusalem, following Jesus on his walk to Calvary. We visited the Mount of Olives, celebrated Holy Communion in the Garden of Gethsemane, visited Lazarus' tomb, saw the Church of the Nativity, the Sea of Galilee, the Dead Sea, the Church of the Holy Sepulchre, and many of the spiritual places associated with the Holy Land.

Even as we visited the scenes of Jesus' life, we were given to understand that we were not actually walking on the physical ground that Jesus trod. There are many levels to the city. Throughout the pages of history the city was built and then demolished; another city was built on top of it. And so we were told that most of the road on which Christ actually walked does not exist above ground. We can only find remnants of it below ground.

But it really did not matter to us. We could still feel Jesus' radiance surrounding us.

Some of Mark Prophet's Embodiments

I have briefly mentioned several of Mark's earlier embodiments—Saint Bonaventure, Longfellow, Ikhnaton and Saladin. Now I would like to put in the proper chronological sequence more of his lifetimes that have been revealed to us. The ones that I will discuss are only a few of Mark's many embodiments—the major ones of which we are aware.

Each soul has major and minor embodiments as she* progresses through time and space. Some lifetimes are for service to the world and some are more private for the main purpose

---

*We use the pronouns she and her to refer to the soul because each soul, whether housed in a male or a female body, is the feminine counterpart of the masculine Spirit.

of learning lessons and balancing karma.

Throughout our journey on the way to our eventual ascension in the light, we have all had thousands of embodiments, in which we lived in many different periods of history and fulfilled many different roles. We have been saints and sinners; we have had lives when we were wealthy and lives when we were paupers; we have had lives of success and lives of failure; lives of beauty and ones of degradation; we have lived in the bodies of children and those of the elderly. We have seen civilizations rise and fall.

Usually a certain embodiment is not revealed to us unless there is some special reason why we should know of it and if we can profit from that knowledge. The masters do not reveal lifetimes to us just to satisfy our curiosity. The reason is so that we can learn lessons from that particular life.

When we receive knowledge of a certain embodiment, either from the master or in meditation with our own Christ Self, we should make fervent calls and prayers to transmute the karma of any negative aspects of that life and also of that period in history.

The masters do not recommend that we visit psychics or fortune-tellers who offer to reveal our past lives. Neither do they recommend hypnosis and past-life regressions. Be content to wait until these lives are revealed to you by inspiration from the masters. Be content to live in the present and try daily to balance your karma so that you can ascend back to the heart of God at the close of this lifetime or at least the next.

We know that Mark Prophet had many embodiments, both in Church and State, which the masters have not yet revealed to us. The earliest memory of Mark that has been shown to us is on Atlantis when he was a priest of the sacred fire* and a master of invocation in the temple there.

He lived as **Lot**, Abraham's brother's son, four thousand years ago. The history of his life in Sodom and Gomorrah and the destruction of the cities of the plain are briefly recorded in early scripture (twelfth through fourteenth chapters of Genesis).

Thirty-three hundred years ago he was the Egyptian Pharaoh **Ikhnaton**, whose previous title was **Amenhotep IV**. He challenged the false priesthood of Thebes and the worship of the pagan god Amon. He established monotheism in Egypt, the worship of the I AM Presence, which to him was Aton (At-one), symbolized in the disk of the Sun. Egypt enjoyed a golden age of art, poetry and music during his reign until he was murdered by the priests of the old religion.

It is said that Moses himself, when he was in Egypt, learned what he knew about monotheism from the teachings and doctrine of Ihknaton and that Moses was a follower of Ihknaton years later.

He was **Aesop** (620–560 B.C.), a Greek slave who won his freedom as a teller of stories and fables. In his tales he stripped people of their disguises and won their hatred. He was eventually murdered by the townspeople.

We have Lanello's own account dictated in a *Pearl of Wisdom** of his life as an **Arabian shepherd boy** in the Syrian foothills of the Middle East. This lifetime was a stepping stone to his becoming a shepherd of souls as Mark Prophet and later the Ascended Master Lanello.

He was **Mark** the evangelist who wrote the account of the works of Jesus in the New Testament as these were told him by Peter the Apostle. His gospel was written in A.D. 68. He was chosen as Peter's chief disciple and scribe. Mark founded the Church at Alexandria, Egypt, where he was later martyred.

Origen of Alexandria (A.D. 185–254) So, here he returns again to Egypt—right back where he left off as Mark, ready to be martyred again, if necessary, for his mission. It is interesting to note the continued reembodiment of the soul in Egypt as Ihknaton and then Mark and now Origen.

He became known as one of the most distinguished theologians of the early Church, setting forth the true teachings of

Jesus Christ on reincarnation and the hierarchy of heavenly beings. But his deeper understanding seemed fanatical and heretical to worldly minds. He was banished from Egypt, imprisoned and later martyred once again.

Origen left behind a massive body of writing, numbering close to one thousand titles. But in the sixth century, his doctrines were no longer taught in the Church, were pronounced anathema and destroyed. Only a few fragments remain today.

Basically the entire teachings of the ascended masters were contained in Origen's writings and have remained hidden in the hearts of his students, even today. Now you may understand why, when you first came upon the teachings, you felt that you already knew them. They rang true and were familiar to you. It is because in some previous incarnation you experienced these teachings, or you may have been studying in the retreats of the masters between physical embodiments.

This list of lifetimes leaves vast centuries where there is no account of when and where Mark lived, and yet we know that he was almost continually incarnating because of the advanced nature of his soul and the ongoing nature of his mission.

As **Clovis,** a Frankish king of the Merovingian dynasty, (A.D. 466–511), he unified much of Roman Gaul to establish the kingdom of a unified France. He married Clothilde, a Christian, and proclaimed Christianity as the religion of France.

His next embodiment that we know of was in the days of King Arthur as **Lancelot du Lac.** Once again he came from France, picking up the previous incarnation of Clovis. His life as Knight Champion of Camelot and Arthur and Guinevere and knight of the Round Table has been told in song and tales around the world.

Saladin was one of the great Moslem leaders, ruling over Egypt, Palestine, Syria and Yemen—much of the Middle East—in the twelfth century. Although a powerful general, Saladin is remembered for his generosity, gentleness, honesty and justice to all people.

Saint Bonaventure, the Seraphic Doctor of the Church, played an important role in the Franciscan Order of the Church in the thirteenth century. (We have already spoken of his embodiment in chapter 9.)

He was also the soul of **Hiawatha,** legendary chief of the Iroquois nation, immortalized in Longfellow's poem *The Song of Hiawatha.*

Louis XIV, *Le Roi Soleil,* was King of France from 1643 to 1715. His was the longest recorded reign in European history. The "Sun King" sought to outpicture his soul memory of the culture of Venus in the magnificent palace and gardens of Versailles.

The beloved poet **Henry Wadsworth Longfellow** (1807–1882), whose poetry captured the hearts of America and Europe, was another of Mark's major embodiments. You can feel the beauty of his soul in *A Psalm of Life, Excelsior* and other of his masterpieces.

Born in Russia at the turn of the century, had Mark survived the Bolshevik Revolution in the early twentieth century, he was destined to unite the children of Mother Russia for a century of enlightened self-rule and the fullest development of the God-potential of the people and the country itself. But it was not to be, as that young life was cut short.

And so, on December 24, 1919, Mark L. Prophet was born in Chippewa Falls, Wisconsin to finish his trek through the ages and the nations of the world. He ascended back to the heart of God on February 26, 1973, as the Ascended Master Lanello.

In living those lives with him, we find that many of his embodiments seem familiar to us. Many of us have been with Mark many times. Souls tend to reembody in groups, and we have been with Mark throughout history as members of his mandala, sharing a common mission and a common goal—to enlighten mankind to the reality of the One God.

CHAPTER ELEVEN

MEMORIES OF LA TOURELLE

SOME OF THE HAPPIEST DAYS of my life—and some of the most serious—were spent as a staff member at La Tourelle. So many episodes come flooding back to my memory as I contemplate the years of my life from 1966 to 1973. And not the least of these is my great joy in having finally found my guru—Mark L. Prophet.

Mark was a true friend and counselor. He was a master psychologist who could read the heart and soul of a person as well as his aura. He was always willing to take the time to offer us the momentum of his self-mastery in the cycles of time and space. Staff life at La Tourelle with Mark was an intimate, almost family experience for us all.

He was fun to be with, and yet often his moments of gaiety could suddenly change to a deep seriousness when, if one listened closely, one could receive deep spiritual truths from the master. El Morya lived in Mark's aura. Mark was a true blue-ray* man with a heart filled with love for the whole world. And that love extended personally to each one of us on staff.

Mark had a warm, personal relationship with everyone he met. And that very openness caused him to be hurt, time and time again, because many misunderstood him. The great light that he carried oftentimes seemed to antagonize some people on contact. And he was always so surprised because he couldn't see what he had done to make them upset.

Nevertheless, Mark never erected barriers or grew a tough skin or a stone wall to protect himself from the type of outrage some people occasionally expressed. He continued to give of

La Tourelle in Colorado Springs

himself to all whom he met. And consequently, at times, he would be deeply hurt, almost like a child who has been rebuffed.

The Frozen Custard Story

One story he used to tell us, his "frozen custard story," explains this perfectly. Mark loved ice cream, especially the soft variety. One afternoon he took several of his friends to an ice cream parlor and ordered frozen custard (as Mark said, "Homemade custard, vanilla flavored and just melting in your mouth"). When the order arrived, there was a large piece of plaster in it that had fallen from the ceiling. You could still see the spot on the ceiling from which it had fallen and you could also see the cobwebs from the ceiling still in the custard.

He called the waitress, pointed out the plaster to her, and

asked for another dish of ice cream. He said, "As you can see, there is something in here." And she said, "Yes, I see it. I'll exchange it for you." Soon the manager came out and berated Mark loudly for trying to ruin his business.

Mark protested, "No, I am certainly not trying to ruin your business. In fact, I was just telling my friends what wonderful custard you make and that is why we came in here." The manager insisted, "No, you are trying to ruin my business."

By that time everybody in the place was agitated, and a scene ensued. As the waitress and other customers rushed loudly to Mark's defense, even pointing out the piece of plaster, the manager became more and more incensed.

The manager said to the poor waitress, "Tell him there was nothing in it." She said, "Oh, but there was. There was a black thing, and the black thing had things coming out of it."

In the midst of all this hubbub, Mark quietly left the ice cream parlor. He had been looking forward to this treat and couldn't possibly imagine what he had done to cause such a commotion.

The only answer to this and similar occurrences seemed to be that the spiritual light* that he bore was overwhelming to some people. They would react negatively on the instant for no apparent reason. Many of us do not realize the amount of light we carry. "It's not what you do," Elizabeth Clare Prophet teaches, "It's simply what you are. It's not what you say; it's simply your Presence that so agitates this certain type of human consciousness."

Four Quarterly Conferences

It was the spirit of Mark that set the geometry for this organization and the four quarterly conferences. These four conferences were held near the changing of the four seasons of the year—at spring and autumn equinox and summer and winter solstice. These conferences were begun in the early years of the movement in Washington D.C., Virginia and Colorado

Mark and Elizabeth during a break at a conference at La Tourelle

Springs. They are still being held today in Park County, Montana and have been held in many cities throughout the United States and once internationally in Mexico City.

The class program is filled with lectures by the messenger and other authorities in their field, dictations* from the ascended masters, instruction for new people and fellowship for all.

Mark related how he came to plan such a full program as we have at present. There is virtually no spare time during the entire duration of a conference. He said that El Morya once corrected him on his format for the classes in the early days of The Summit. Mark said that he would schedule about two dictations a day, sometimes only one. He would have a short service in the morning at about eleven o'clock and maybe nothing more until four in the afternoon and then again in the evening at eight o'clock.

It turned out that the students would go downtown to Washington, D.C., become entangled in a whirlwind of shopping and other activities and even attend an occasional movie, instead of returning for the next conference event.

Mark said, "The master said to me, 'You're having a little problem.' And I said, 'Yes, sir.' Morya answered, 'Well, let's keep the children busy. We'll have a fuller program so that they will have something more to do. And now you are going to have to lecture part of the time.'"

Mark's Lectures

So that is how Mark began lecturing on spiritual topics in addition to taking dictations from the ascended masters. Mark's lectures became so interesting that people soon lost their desire to shop or attend movies while the conference was in progress. They did not want to miss a minute of it. And thus was born our intensive program for classes lasting anywhere from four to ten days. Some students even mentioned that they enjoyed Mark's lectures as much or more than the dictations of the masters.

One observation that many of us had about Mark's lectures was that he seemed to have an uncanny ability to know just exactly what everyone in the audience needed to hear. So often someone would comment, "I had this problem, this burden on my heart, and Mark tuned in and knew exactly what to say. He answered my unspoken question." He could just look over the audience and seem to sense their problems and the Holy Spirit provided the perfect answer. Mark was deeply concerned about reaching people where they were.

I don't believe Mark really realized how closely he was connected to the Holy Spirit. As a child he had received all nine gifts of the Holy Spirit mentioned in the Bible. Paul's preaching about these gifts is recorded in the twelfth chapter of the first Epistle to the Corinthians: the word of wisdom, the word of knowledge, faith, gifts of healing, the working of miracles, prophecy, discerning of spirits, speaking in tongues and interpretation of tongues.

He had great attunement with the inner realms of light while still keeping his feet firmly planted on the ground.

Mark was a firm believer in teaching just a little at a time and giving the student's Inner Self time to process the teachings that had been received. He felt that this method was far better than overwhelming a new student with more than they could comprehend at one time.

I remember I once was quite concerned about not being able to take down in my notes everything he said. I told Mark that I was worried about not being able to remember everything from his lecture or the master's dictation.

He said, "Don't worry, dear heart, your soul knows, and it is the soul the masters are teaching. Remember that the brain is not the mind. The brain is only the instrument which the Christ Self uses to anchor the Mind of God in the planes of matter." I was comforted to a certain degree, but I was still burdened by the gems that fell from his lips that I was missing.

I seem to have a very logical, sequential type of mind, and there was one aspect of Mark's lectures that disturbed me occasionally. I know now, years later, after I have had an opportunity to study the transcripts of his lectures, that he was using this tool for a purpose.

Mark would announce the title of his lecture, begin to speak on that topic for a few moments and then digress on a multitude of other subjects, anecdotes and miscellany. I was expecting the material to be presented in a logical sequence that further explained the title. I was always anxiously waiting for him to return to his subject.

I had known that Mark could read minds and auras, but one day it was brought home to me very personally and to my embarrassment. In the midst of an interesting lecture, as usual continually off the subject and in front of the entire audience, Mark said, "Yes, Mrs. Booth, I'll come back to my subject in a minute. Please be patient." In that instant I would have been grateful if the earth could have opened and swallowed me up or at least if I could have crawled beneath my chair out of sight. You have heard how Mark interspersed his serious lectures with anecdotes and jokes to hold people's attention and also to teach a lesson. Case in point was his "parrot joke."

I am going to relate it to you in Mark's own words. I could not possibly tell it any better. At a very serious point in one lecture he digressed and said, "Now, in the midst of all this I would like to tell you a little story. It seems that it was the occasion of a man and his wife's wedding anniversary. And so, he decided that he would go downtown and buy her something that would please her. As he was going by a pet store, he decided upon a parrot.

"So, he brought the parrot home. And it had two strings, one on each leg as it stood on its perch. He said to his wife, 'Now, you pull the left-hand string.' So she pulled the left-hand string and the parrot said, 'Happy Anniversary, darling!'

"They were quite delighted with this. And he said to her, 'Now pull the other string.' So she pulled the right string and the parrot said, 'Good morning. It's a nice day.'

"About that time, the wife turned to him and said, 'Why don't you pull both strings?'

"The parrot looked up at both of them, turned to the man and said, 'You idiot! If you pull both strings, I'll fall off my perch!'"

And Mark continued, "So today, I suspect that many people would like to pull both my strings so I'd fall off my perch right now—telling a story like that after such a sublime statement that preceded it! Nevertheless, I think that sometimes we need to relax because the world is far too tense."

Babaji's Radiation

Mark was a great master of meditation, both in this life and in former ones. He had a close tie to the Five Dhyani Buddhas* and could go into samadhi* effortlessly. One of the lovely surprises we were allowed at certain conferences was a moment when Mark would become very still, take a deep breath, and you could feel a great ripple of light flow through the room.

The first time I experienced this, Mark said, "Did anybody feel anything?" I did not know what he expected us to feel, but my heart just about leaped out of my chest. Since I did not raise my hand, Mark said, "Mrs. Booth, did you feel anything?" I answered, "Well, yes. I think so. But what was it?" He said that he had contacted Babaji, one of the great unascended masters of the Himalayas, and that that radiation was Babaji's greeting to us.

Every few conferences after that, in the midst of Mark's lectures, he would contact Babaji, and you could tangibly feel his light. I remember one time I was out in the kitchen making peanut butter sandwiches for our snack bar. Soon I heard over the intercom, "How many felt Babaji? Did anyone in the kitchen feel the radiation? I want everybody who felt Babaji to come in." So here I am with my apron on saying, "Yes, Mark, I felt Babaji." Mark was definitely connected with the great masters of the Himalayas and the Buddhas.

Mark explained that there are many ways in which a student can experience radiation—when they are praying or decreeing, when they are meditating, when they experience the radiation of an ascended master in his dictation, or even in moments of high attunement with the beauties of nature. He said that this radiation can be felt in the beginning as a tingle of light in the chakras* or hands, or there may be a warmth spreading over the body as waves of light.

By way of giving us a bit of encouragement, Mark said that for years and years he never felt so much as a tiny bit of radiation. And then, he said, he would feel just a little thrill that would come through the air. Sometimes it would land around his heart and would rise up until he could feel it in his head center, or crown chakra. Sometimes other centers of his body would glow and vibrate with this tremendous feeling. And then, one day when he was meditating deeply on God, the walls

The Messengers at the altar at La Tourelle

of the room seemed to melt away and he seemed to be in a great tunnel in which light and radiation were pouring down on him.

A Treat at the End of a Conference

It was Mark who took the brunt of most of the lectures and dictations during a class. Elizabeth usually gave one lecture and one dictation and led our decree services, but Mark was responsible for most of the program. She was busy with four young children and with writing *Climb the Highest Mountain*. So, often on the last day of the conference his voice would be quite hoarse.

When we would see him enter the room wearing around his throat a violet silk scarf that he'd bought in India, we knew we were going to have a treat. He would ask one of the staff to go to his office and bring him his book of Longfellow's poems. I have never tired of hearing him read from *The Song of Hiawatha* in his beautiful voice, even though it was a bit husky by now. This seemed to be his way of relaxation after a long conference. I can hear him yet:

> By the shores of Gitche Gumee,
> By the shining Big-Sea-Water,
> Stood the wigwam of Nokomis,
> Daughter of the Moon, Nokomis.
> Dark behind it ran the forest,
> Rose the black and gloomy pine-trees,
> Rose the firs with cones upon them;
> Bright before it beat the water,
> Beat the clear and sunny water,
> Beat the shining Big-Sea-Water.

And at other times Mark would read:

> All your strength is in your union,
> All your danger is in discord;
> Therefore be at peace henceforward,
> And as brothers live together.

These sessions always meant so much to us because in a previous life Mark was Professor Longfellow.

Tell Them

I remember one night at the close of a conference when Mark asked me to come into his office. (I was not on staff yet.) He told me about the many years that he and Elizabeth had been working on the manuscript of *Climb the Highest Mountain,* and now it was nearing completion.

This book had to be written during odd moments that they could find while still performing the duties of messengers—the daily responsibilities of a worldwide organization, having a large staff, and publishing the weekly *Pearls of Wisdom* and monthly Keepers of the Flame lessons.

Mark told me that he wanted to read me a poem that he had just written for inclusion in the book. I can still remember his beautiful voice and the cadences that seemed to bring back to the twentieth century the voice of Longfellow's *Song of Hiawatha.*

Tell Them

Tell them,
Ancient Fires,
How the strata of the rock
Cooled and formed the surface
Of a verdant sphere to be.

Tell them,
Ancient Waters,
Of the coolants of the deep—
Mighty cycles of perfection,
Marine world now we see.

Tell them,
Mighty Atmosphere,
Of blue inspired veil,
Of lacy white cloud cover
Curtained Cosmos does unveil.

Tell them of Creation
That like clockwork telling time
Shows the intricacy of nature
In a network so sublime.

Tell them of a seedling
Filled with patterned destiny.
Tell them of a cedar tall
That through sunshine was to be.

Tell them of a whisper
That was heard within the soul.
Tell them, Ageless Wisdom,
Nature's blessed goal.

Tell them of Reality
That plays hide and seek with men.
Tell them of a Golden Age
That cometh once again.

Tell them of the Buddha
And of Christ upon the hill.
Tell them Truth, Reality
That hungry souls do fill.

Tell them of electric spark
That flashes 'cross the sky.
Speak of Immortality
    that cradles our humanity—
That one day none shall die.

Speak of Truth
That out the mouth of Christ did manifest,
That Pilate heard and questioned,
That now in truth is blessed.

Speak it loud and speak it long;
Tell in poetry and song
That tall upon the hills of time
An ageless wisdom now does chime—

Carillon bells from celestial towers
Rung by other hands than ours,
Angel voices chiming in
Raise an anthem now to win.

Tell them how that we who read
Can in faith plant vital seed,
Watch them push their shoots right through
Soil and rock and obstacle too—

Thrusting roots into the earth,
Seeking vital essence' worth
And reaching to the sun to claim
That I AM real in God's own Name!

Tell them, then, that darkest night
Waits the first dawn's early light,
That man may see and catch the thought

Mark L. Prophet

That God in truth has to us brought
An opportunity so fair—
An answer to a child's own prayer.

Our Father, help us now to be
Selflessly engraft' in Thee—
That our nature then shall be
Like a father's heart of love;

Seeds from heaven up above
Scattered here in garden fair—
Sun and rain in falling there
Can assist the planned delight
And the victory for the right!

Tell them, Father, Ageless One,
Of Thy Nature's Golden Sun.
Tell them of Thy Name and Spirit!
Tell them so that all may hear it!
Tell them so that none may fear it!
Tell them so that all revere it!
Tell them so that none may lose
Life or gift—that all may choose
Now and without fail to see
That only Truth can ever be
Clad with Immortality.

The Snack Bar

You remember in chapter 9 how I described the snack bar that we provided during meals and breaks in Santa Barbara. Well, it became so successful and well liked that Mark suggested we do the same thing at La Tourelle during conferences. Although there were many restaurants nearby in Colorado Springs, when the people attending the conferences went down to Nevada Avenue for their meals, it often took several hours for them to return. Our afternoon schedules were disrupted as a result.

Since we were vegetarians at the time, our menu never varied and was the same as served at the Motherhouse—rice, soup, sandwiches, apple juice and tea. By Sunday, the last day of the conference, I said to the young man helping me in the kitchen, "This is nonsense. Nobody is going to eat rice, soup and sandwiches for the fifth day in a row. They will all go downtown to a restaurant for a Sunday dinner."

We had something like fourteen little leftover peanut butter and jelly sandwiches and a tiny bowl of rice. I said, "This is it. I'm not going to cook today. We'll just put these few left-overs out because most people will go downtown for an Easter dinner today."

The dictation from Jesus was announced and we all went into the sanctuary. For some reason Mark seated me right in the front row, directly across from him. To this day I don't know what the dictation was about because suddenly Jesus said, "I am inviting every one of you to stay and have lunch with me here at La Tourelle."

If you have ever seen absolute panic, that described my state of consciousness at that moment. Here I was, sitting in the middle of the front row, so I couldn't possibly go back into the kitchen and make some more peanut butter and jelly sand-wiches to feed this group.

I kept saying, "Jesus, you've got to do this. I have only four-teen peanut butter and jelly sandwiches. I can't feed all these people. You have got to do it for me. You fed the five thousand in Galilee with five loaves and two fishes. You invited these people today, and I don't know how to feed them. Don't even show me how. Just do it!"

When I saw Mark after the dictation, I said, "Mark, why did you do this to me? I told you in advance that I did not have any food today and you agreed that they should go to a restau-rant for a good Easter dinner." Mark replied, "Mrs. Booth, I did not do anything. It was Jesus' dictation."

My rather rebellious answer was, "All right, then, I'll cut my fourteen sandwiches in half and that will be twenty-eight sandwiches. I have enough rice for about three people and enough soup for about two servings. When it is all gone, they can just go down to Nevada Avenue and eat." Mark just looked through me and said, "Jesus wants everybody to eat here."

I had never imagined that one hundred and fifty people could make such a long line. It seemed to stretch on and on and on forever. The staff who were taking money were letting people buy *two* sandwiches or even as many as they wanted.

They were even coming back for second helpings of peanut butter and jelly sandwiches and rice and soup. And everyone was saying this was the most delicious meal they had ever tasted.

Jesus knew how to precipitate again in 1970 just as he had 2000 years ago. I knew, then, that the days of miracles are not over.

I was sitting happily in the chapel after the luncheon thinking, "Well isn't that nice. Jesus did it again." My reverie was broken by Mark's announcement, "Mrs. Booth has something to tell you." I said, "What am I supposed to say?" Mark answered, "Jesus would like you to come up here and tell us about your lunch." And so, I had an opportunity to tell everyone that their lunch had been precipitated for them by Jesus.

Dictations

Dictations are messages transmitted from the ascended masters to their chosen messengers.* Those who are the ascended masters' authentic messengers have been trained for many embodiments for this office in hierarchy.*

Mark explained several forms whereby the masters transmit their dictations. One way is similar to a telegraph. He said that you see the letters passing in front of you. They sort of pass in review in your mind and you read them with the spiritual part of your being. The Spirit reads the letters, but they are not visible to your physical eyes. They are visible only within. At other times the masters physically take over the messenger's body and speak through him—*ex cathedra* dictations, these are called.

A messenger is not a channel, not a spiritualistic medium; a messenger comes under the dispensation of the prophets. In every age the Brotherhood has had those who are called the witnesses. These are they who write down the law, who give the warning and who give the prophecy to the people.

God has never left mankind without messengers, without prophets. And they have gone basically unrecognized, unheeded while civilization and karma have taken their course.

The training to be a messenger takes place over thousands of years. It is not something you get by psychic studies, nor is it something you receive by your own effort. The office of the messenger is an assignment and an ordination.

The messenger is never in a trance during a dictation. This is not a form of spiritualism and he has no contact with departed spirits. He has full command of his senses and is in a state of heightened awareness and deep concentration, but never in a trance state. And yet, at this time, he is extremely conscious of vibrations in the room.

There is a very delicate thread of contact between the messenger and the master who is dictating. It is difficult to maintain that thread of contact when someone in the room falls asleep or lets his mind wander. Mark must screen out the thoughts he receives from such people in order to hold contact with the master.

Mark has told us that he was so sensitive that he was like a deep-dish radio telescope that picks up minute vibrations from afar and magnifies them. He said that he could tell what everyone in the room was thinking. It was like picking up 50 or 100 or 200 radio stations all at once. Meanwhile it was imperative that he "tune out" or ignore these vibrations in order to hold his concentration firmly anchored on the ascended master who was dictating.

He could hear a fly walk on the ceiling, could see what was happening in Rome at any given moment, and when he looked at a person he could see all their organs and their skeleton. At one time Mark told us that during a dictation he was in such a heightened state of awareness that he could even hear an ant's footstep in the room.

He said that the words of the dictation come through like a high-speed computer at the same time that someone is moving his chair or there are other distractions in the room. At times Mark would be concerned because he feared his delivery of the master's words may not have been as perfect as he would have liked. At that moment he was trying to overcome the confusion in the room and screen out the thoughts of the audience at the same time as he was trying to hold on to the hand of the master. Thoughts of the audience were often louder than the radiation of the master coming to him through space.

Many times students have received answers from the masters during a dictation even though this person had never asked the question audibly and he had only formed it in his mind. The unusual thing is that several people have often remarked, "That dictation was just for me personally—no one else but me." There must be many tracks to a dictation, and these different tracks reach different people according to their individual need. Each one receives a different kind of therapy.

One thing that often amazed the audience was the power of Mark's voice when an ascended master speaks through him. He says that the volume is regulated by the amount of spiritual energy the master is releasing. Mark has absolutely no control over it, and often it is beyond the power of the human voice to sustain that volume.

When Archangel Michael would begin his dictation with "Hail!" it was almost all we could do to keep from jumping out of our seats. The radiation contained in the volume of the master's release can actually cut a person free from some unwanted adhesion in consciousness, almost like a surgeon with his scalpel. This may free you from some of the psychic effluvia you may be carrying. It may also be an assist toward your ascension.

Several students have mentioned that the recording heads of their tape recorders were burned up by a recording of the master's power and energy. The men in the repair shop were amazed and said they had never before witnessed anything similar. They were curious as to what was being played on the recorder.

Another woman who lived in an apartment house turned the volume down very low so as not to bother the neighbors. She reports that it was turned down almost to a whisper when the tenant from upstairs called and asked her to please turn off her radio. She said that she could feel the vibration that was coming up through her floor.

There is a current, an energy, a radiation to the masters' releases that is completely different from volume, and this penetrates no matter how low the instrument is turned. It still carries authority when it is heard and can still be felt. The penetration of the dictations is very, very powerful.

Sunday Services

Mark always conducted two services on Sunday—one in the morning and one in the evening. Those on Sunday morning were private services for the staff only, during which Mark would receive a live dictation from one of the masters. He would also give us transcendent teachings on subjects that were more advanced and esoteric than those he presented in his evening services. We were very blessed to receive these pearls of wisdom from the lips of such an adept as Mark. Some of his sermons were so transcendent that they took us on a cosmic tour up into higher realms, higher octaves of the cosmos, then brought us back again. It was indeed magnificent!

On Sunday evenings, Mark invited the entire population of Colorado Springs to his public services. Unfortunately, very few accepted his invitation. His sermons on Sunday evening were geared for new people. He never knew who would walk in the door, or if anyone would. He was able to give his congregation, in a matter of just about half an hour, a complete and down-to-earth summary of the teachings of the ascended masters.

He wanted them to know that they have lived before, that they have a destiny, a contact with God, their own individualized I AM Presence, that there is a Great White Brotherhood,* there are ascended masters and that you can make your ascension if you TRY.

Mark's services were very easily understood and he sincerely tried to give each one in his audience just what they needed. In the evenings he played a tape of the morning's live dictation. However, on occasion, groups of neighbors would come just to see "what is going on and what kind of people live here." Mark had a special way of inviting them to leave, without actually saying so.

I remember one time when Mark suddenly stopped his service and said, "Let's sing a song." And we sang. And we sang. And we sang. Suddenly three people in the front row got up and walked out. Mark said, "Now that that is taken care of, let's return to our service and our dictation." He said, "You know, these people did not really want to be here, and I had to find a way to let them leave graciously."

The best way I can sum up Mark's services is to tell you about his sermon entitled, "Waves Upon the Sea." It was on a Sunday night, at the end of a five-day conference, and Mark was tired. In walked twelve to fifteen new people from Colorado Springs, dressed very stylishly and interested in "checking us out." This was in March 1967 and I was not a staff member yet. Mark related the following story to me as I was preparing to go back home to California.

I thought this was the most beautiful service I had ever experienced, but Mark said, "I came as near to panicking as I ever have. I said, 'Morya, I just can't do it. I'm too tired.' Morya answered, 'Don't worry Mark. We'll help you.'" This sermon remains in my memory as the most transcendent I have ever heard anywhere. The masters told the entire story of the teachings in only about twenty minutes, in a manner that absolutely thrilled the guests. All Mark could say was, "All glory to God!"

The closing words of his lecture were: "I shall say no more on this subject now. I shall close the door upon it. But I pray that those of you who are receptive to the light that God is will open the doors of your hearts and ponder well upon these thoughts. For they are not my own, but they come from a Higher Source."

Mark asked me to come into his office before I left so that he could explain the service. When he asked how I liked the sermon, I said that I really did not know if it was a lecture or a dictation. I started taking notes until the radiation became so intense that I stopped.

He explained what El Morya meant when he said, "Don't worry, Mark. We'll help you." He said this was a lecture from the seven chohans, the lords of the seven rays.* He said it was just as though a glyph of light descended over his third eye and the entire lecture was precipitated instantly.

This was a moment in time to which I keep returning whenever I hear the recording of that service that took place thirty years ago.

Fireside Chats

And then, following the Sunday service we were all invited to meet with Mark in the family room to enjoy one of his fireside chats. After the evening services there were about ten or fifteen minutes of tea and cookies in the rotunda, where people could talk or browse through the books and tapes that were available for sale.

Following this period of fellowship we would all go into the family room and Mark would preside at his weekly fireside chat. The room would be filled to capacity—people seated on the couches, standing against the wall and seated on the floor.

Mark was always the genial host. He thoroughly enjoyed meeting new people. These fireside chats were an excellent way of immediately integrating new people into our group. No one was a stranger to Mark. We all looked forward to these moments with Mark as the highlight of our week.

The family room was beautifully decorated, and on chilly nights you could always expect to find a crackling fire blazing in the fireplace. This was a time when anyone was free, in this informal setting, to ask Mark any question concerning the teachings. We enjoyed not only his answers but also the anecdotes with which he was accustomed to peppering his teachings. Even now, many years after his transition, we can still see and hear Mark recounting his stories. Unconditional love was what we felt from this man. And we all remember his wonderful, powerful, loving and firm handshake.

Staff Meetings

Those of us who lived back at La Tourelle with Mark will never forget his staff meetings. Each Monday morning at nine o'clock we would all meet in the chapel for an hour with him. This was a time for inspiration, instruction and surprises.

I had the experience of knowing a true Guru in the person of Mark Prophet. He was most unpredictable, moving freely with the winds of the Holy Spirit. You could never tie him down. You could never stereotype him. You could never label him. And just when you had come to believe that you finally understood him, Mark would do a complete turnaround and surprise you again.

Mark has told us in many different messages that the path of the true chela* is the most difficult, the most arduous, the most painful and challenging of any calling you can take up in life on earth.

He was a true Zen* master to whom nothing and everything was sacred. He was a man of faith, an example of living faith. Mark expressed his creed of belief to us in one meeting. He said, "One of the qualities of my own life that I would like to communicate to you is that I have absolute faith in the invulnerability of God, in the plans of God, in the outworkings of God and his intent to keep me in the hollow of his hand. And I believe he can do it for everybody else, too.

"I believe that inside of me there is a spark. I believe that spark, or that flame, or whatever it is, is a part of God now, always has been a part of God and always will be. And I believe that God is going to keep me as I tie myself with all of my heart to that spark and blend with it until ultimately I become that flame." Mark derived his great power from dipping deeply into the love flame in his heart.

There were few problems of discord and disobedience when we were living with Mark. For one reason, we all lived as a closely-knit family—a true community. However, Mark said that he had been admonished by the masters not to be completely lenient with people. Mark was fair but strict.

He would brook no lapse of discipline in the staff. He believed that where there is discipline, there is love—true divine love, not the gooey, mushy kind so often mistaken for love.

Mark felt that the greatest love is the love that tries to bring people into a regimen that will someday eventually bring the greatest freedom to those people. His type of discipline was meant to help the staff find order and reason in their lives.

Of course, Mark Prophet could be very firm. He could be very loud, but he was never discordant, even when he was loud. When he said, "Woman!" with the full power of his voice, you wanted to crawl under the nearest table.

You felt the power of God stripping you of your human creation. It was a shattering experience, but only shattering to your human creation and ego. And, believe you me, we learned! No matter how serious the experience, Mark always saw to it that the soul was comforted.

He used to say that the proper method of discipline is to make a "sandwich": (1) express your concern to the person over the infraction, (2) explain the infraction of the law in no uncertain terms and describe the penalty, (3) leave them feeling that you care about them.

Sometimes, after a blistering exposé of our actions, Mark would put his arm around our shoulders and say, "Now you understand why I had to do this, don't you?"

These staff meetings became a source of enlightenment, wisdom, humor, teaching and discipline. Daily events were discussed and decisions were made on everything—down to the smallest detail of our life on staff. Everyone had a chance to have his or her say. Mark would always listen to the staff and try to get the best information about any given situation before he made a final decision.

I used to question his views on discipline so that I could be a better administrator at the Motherhouse in Santa Barbara. Burning toast was one thing that disturbed Mark's acute sense of smell. A person would put a piece of bread in the toaster and then wander off to do something else in the meantime and forget that he was making toast. In a few minutes the fragrance of burnt toast would be wafting throughout the entire building.

One time I said, "Mark, you are constantly assessing one dollar fines. Why? It doesn't do the least bit of good." He answered, "Yes, Mrs. Booth, you're absolutely right, it doesn't. But when people actually pay the fine, they are paying the karma for that incident. In this way it doesn't have to accrue to their karmic record." (And still, the toast kept burning.)

Mark was a very practical man—especially concerning little details. He felt that the teachings would be of no value if they weren't made practical. And yet, Mark's consciousness could also soar to untrammeled heights in an instant.

He was constantly admonishing us to turn off the lights when we left a room. After one staff meeting when he made such a point of this subject, I asked Mark, "Why? Why spend so much energy on such a mundane subject?" He said that I could be sure that anytime he was belaboring the subject with us it was because El Morya was getting after him about it.

He said that electricity is light precipitated from the sun and El Morya had to go before the Karmic Board to receive new grants of light for The Summit Lighthouse. Morya had to prove to the Lords of Karma* how well we had used our last dispensation and had not wasted electricity, as energy, among other things. Mark said, "Anytime I lecture you, you can be sure that El Morya is worrying me."

While we are on the subject of attention to small details, we had an entire staff meeting on the proper way to *close doors.* I have already related how sensitive Mark was to sound and vibrations. When someone would allow a door to slam, that sound would jar Mark's consciousness.

One day he took the entire staff and visibly showed us the correct way to close a door. We were supposed to keep our hand on the knob until the door was completely closed and not let it slam by itself as we were walking away. Can you imagine the picture? Here we were, standing in line and watching each other, one by one, closing a door properly. I can tell you that this little exercise remains in my mind today every time I have occasion to close a door.

At another time we had a rather unusual staff meeting as a result of one of El Morya's requests. He said, "Mark, tell the staff that everything must be done! Now, go and have a staff meeting on that subject." He said that the man who is mowing the lawns is as vital to this organization as the messenger who gives the dictations. If the lawns were not mowed and there were no one to mow them, the messenger would have to spend his time mowing the lawn. The lady who is putting toilet tissue in the bathroom is vital because otherwise the messenger would have to stop his work to go find toilet tissue.

The staff meetings became a never-ending source of instruction and surprises to us. One morning Mark buzzed five times on the intercom for all of us to assemble. Without any preamble, he said. "I want each one of you to take your shoes off and let me sniff them." As we marched before him, one by one, each one holding their shoes up for his inspection, he would say, "Not bad," or "Oh, this one needs a little powder." Finally, at the end, as a word of explanation, Mark said, "El Morya told me to do this and that it was a matter of humility for me." Well, I could never decide if it was a matter of humility for Mark or for us. Remember, I told you previously that Mark and Morya were both Zen masters.

How often have I heard Mark say to someone who had just "spaced out" and acted irrationally, "You are a *tool*." He meant that by not concentrating and instead letting our consciousness idle in neutral, the negative force had been able to ride in and take over our actions. He said they could project a stupefying ray on us.

But by no means were all our staff meetings on such mundane subjects. We were often privileged to receive some of the most magnificent and transcendent instruction on the planet. Mark could take a recent book he had read or an article on almost any subject and transform it into an electrifying experience by giving the esoteric meaning behind it. We learned so much from his own meditations on the subject.

One such book he endorsed was Og Mandino's *The Greatest Salesman in the World*. Mark's philosophy was that he actually enjoyed the success of other people and was in no way jealous or unduly concerned with any measure of his own success. His credo was, "O God, make me a better instrument of your faith and your peace and your love and tell me what I can do for you." He felt that by studying Og Mandino's book we could all apply his principles of successful and victorious living in our own lives. Mark held a series of meetings where he would read one chapter of the book and discuss with us some of the deeper meanings of the teachings it contained.

"Kitchen Meetings"

An extension of staff meetings seemed to just "happen" at night with Mark and the men in the kitchen. I don't think they were really planned—they just happened. Mark would go into the kitchen to have a snack late at night just to unwind from the pressures of the day. And, then, almost instantly from nowhere it seemed, men would find some reason why they needed to be in the kitchen.

Mark enjoyed these informal meetings with his men, and they were certainly grateful for his presence with them. There ensued little vignettes on politics, current affairs, the state of the world and other timely subjects. It was a very personal encounter, and the men just loved it. The women often wished that they could attend also, but we knew that these times were reserved for just the men with Mark

Of course, there were also times when the women were happy not to be a part of these nightly meetings. These were the "wrestling matches" that often occurred in the kitchen late at night. Mark would wrestle with the human consciousness, and he would not give up on anybody. But often he would physically wrestle, much to the men's delight. All of a sudden any man might find himself literally on the floor of the kitchen. At one time, after a particularly spirited match, Mark said, " I just beat ten-thousand years of karma out of you."

Health and Fitness

Toward the latter years of his life, Mark developed an interest in health and physical fitness. He often fasted and recommended that certain staff members fast with him. He made vitamins and supplements available to all who could not afford them. In fact, he often put bottles of specific nutrients on the table for all who wished to avail themselves of these supplements.

Mark joined a health spa and gave gift memberships to certain men who could not afford the monthly payments. Night after night he would trudge off to the spa with his friends.

Mark's mother would never allow him to learn to swim as a child. She had come close to drowning once, herself, and so she had an overpowering fear of the water and of losing her only son if she allowed him to swim. Now, at the age of fifty-four, Mark took up swimming lessons at the European Health Spa. I remember the look of triumph on his face as he told us, "Guess what? I swam the length of the pool today."

In fact, so interested was Mark in health and purification that he installed a sauna at La Tourelle. Someone gave him a gift of $1,000, and he decided that the best way he could use it would be for the staff. Many of the young men who came to join at this time had just come off drugs and needed these measures of purification so that their bodies could detoxify.

Mark, as well as some of the men, took Karate and Aikido lessons at a local school for the martial arts. We could often see them on a Sunday afternoon practicing their exercises on the back lawn. Mark used to be a yoga instructor in his earlier years and also endorsed this method of exercise, meditation and contemplation. However, he told us that he made greater spiritual progress through the use of the violet transmuting flame* and decrees* than through his ten years of yogic meditation.

Mark loved to eat at restaurants. It seemed to be a relaxation for him. But at this time, he had the staff men experimenting with him on becoming vegetarians. It seemed to him that the only thing you could eat at a restaurant in those days that was vegetarian was cheese. (This was before the present interest in nutrition and low-fat, high-carbohydrate dishes.) I remember Mark saying, "If I eat any more cheese, I'm going to turn into a mouse."

My Rice Fast

Mark was always interested in fasting, and since I was eager to maintain my weight loss, he often invited me to fast for a few days at a time with him.

The one he chose this time was the ten-day rice fast. For ten days we were supposed to eat nothing but brown rice and drink nothing but herb tea. This fast was supposed to bring greater clarity to the mind and health to the body. We began our fast at breakfast time with a small bowl of brown rice and tea. I was happy to notice that I was not hungry and felt fine as the days progressed. At breakfast on day eight, Mark asked me how I felt. I replied that I felt fine, as usual. Mark said that he was beginning to feel "funny" and was going to end his fast. He told me that I could continue so long as I remained close to him so that he could watch my aura.

At lunch on day eight, Mark broke his fast by eating steamed vegetables and rice. And there was my normal bowl of rice and cup of tea at my place. He asked me again how I felt and my answer was, *"Fine!"* I was riding high on the clouds by that time. Mark immediately grabbed the bowl of sesame tahini on the table and poured it over my rice. He also started spooning grape sugar into my tea. When I remonstrated that these foods were not on my fast, he said, "No, they certainly are not, and neither are you on a fast anymore."

I was amazed, but every time I would say anything, Mark would immediately put more food in my bowl and tell me to eat it. He said that he could tell by the inflections of my voice and by reading my aura that I had fasted until I was now out of my body, no longer tethered to earth. All that I knew was that I felt *fine!*

Mark asked me what work I had been doing that morning. I couldn't remember a thing I had done except it seemed that I had spent the time walking up our flights of marble stairs all day. Mark was disgusted and said, "Mrs. Booth, you weren't walking. You were *floating* up those stairs." And he put a lot more food in my bowl and told me to eat it.

I was completely at a loss to know why Mark was angry with me. Mark's answer was, "Because Morya is angry with me." El Morya said that, before I took embodiment, I had promised the master that I would stay in my body this time and work. And Mark said that he had allowed me to get out of my body and float up into the etheric realm again.

All of this was a big surprise to me. All I knew was that I felt *fine!* Mark elicited a solemn promise from me, right on the spot, that I would never fast on rice again. He said that when people fast, often so many toxins are released as a result of the fast, that they are plunged into the astral plane temporarily. But he said that apparently I relate in just the opposite way and go heavenward.

Any fasting I ever did in the future was just for a few days on juice and not on rice. The ascended masters do not recommend fasts of longer duration than three days unless one is directly under the supervision of an adept or guru, (which of course I was). And yet, I still got into trouble.

The Four Winds Organic Center

Mark opened the Four Winds on June 1, 1972, in downtown Colorado Springs.

As I said earlier, the Four Winds was a restaurant, a bookstore, a health food juice bar, and in the back a bakery where we made organic baked goods—pies, breads, etc. And did Mark love the blueberry pie, especially with ice cream!

He chose the name from the reference in Matt. 24:31, "And he shall send his angels with a great sound of a trumpet, and they shall gather together his elect from the four winds,

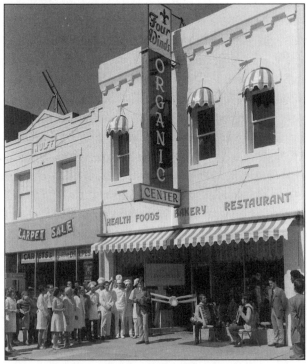

Opening day Four Winds Organic Center

from one end of heaven to the other."

He knew that the residue of pesticides and herbicides in the food were not good for people on the spiritual path. And so he opened the Four Winds Organic Center, determined to provide good wholesome food, organically grown, for all who were interested in nutrition and health.

We even had many of the vegetables, and carrots that were used for our carrot juice, shipped in from California. Our organically grown Kona coffee came direct from Hawaii.

Mark was very proud of his Four Winds. It gave him an excellent opportunity to meet the people of Colorado Springs on an informal basis. He had a special knack for making the customers feel welcome when they came in. He would personally greet them at the door. Sometimes he would sit with them at the juice bar, talk to them, ask them about themselves and their families and just get to know them in a friendly, relaxed atmosphere.

He always seemed to know just where a person was in their level of spiritual development, and he was able to lead them to the next step on the Path through his conversation with them. He loved people and was always interested in what they had to say. He was able to communicate this love and interest to all who came in the door.

The Four Winds became a very popular place for people to gather in Colorado Springs, and it definitely reflected the magnanimous heart of Mark Prophet.

I asked one young man in particular to describe his memories of the Four Winds and Mark Prophet to me. He said, "Who was Mark Prophet to me then? Well, to begin with, in many ways he just appeared to be a regular guy. The day I met him I was sitting at the counter of the juice bar, on one of those heavy cast-iron-base stools, when he just sidled up to me, sat down, and asked, 'Well, how do you like the place?' I don't remember my exact response but I do remember that the place felt alive and that it welcomed me. I looked up at the ceiling painted in a beautiful shade of violet and I felt comfortable and at home there. I kept thinking to myself, 'Hey, I know this guy. I've seen him somewhere.' And so I found my friend Mark again in this lifetime, and he found me.

"He was the regular guy who could meet you on the street and speak to you in your language, right where you were. I don't remember his ever telling me that he was the messenger for the Great White Brotherhood or any of the other specifics regarding his high and holy mission.

"Mark was simply the cup of cool water to a thirsty soul who had lots of questions. He always provided incredible answers in response. I remember thinking to myself how expansive his answers seemed to be. His knowledge was vast. He never appeared to be stumped by any question asked of him."

There was always beautiful classical music playing— Mozart, Beethoven, Vivaldi. Mark especially liked Vivaldi's "Four Seasons" and Pachelbel's "Canon in D." In the middle of the store we had a reading room where customers could browse through the teachings of the ascended masters and sign up for the *Pearls of Wisdom** and the Keepers of the Flame Fraternity.* The Four Winds became a major outreach activity for our organization. Many people first contacted The Summit Lighthouse through our reading room there.

Our Lord said, "Whosoever shall not receive the kingdom of God as a little child, he shall not enter therein."(Mark 10:15) Mark had that childlike state of consciousness you observe in children. That is why he was so much fun to be around—spontaneous and humorous. He could always find something funny in just about anything that happened.

For example, we had a rule that staff were not allowed to hitchhike. Well, one day a staff member missed his ride to the Four Winds, which was in downtown Colorado Springs. And so, he hitchhiked a ride to get to work on time. Just as he was getting out of the car, the driver turned around and punched him in the nose.

The teaching that Mark gave us about this incident was that this was instant karma for the young man's disobedience to the rules of the messenger.

There was one other important function that the Four Winds served: it became a haven for "hippies." During these years, many young people were searching for a meaning to life, for a guru who could teach them. They would arrive at the front door of the Four Winds with their long hair and a pack on their back—searching. And meeting Mark Prophet seemed to fill that void for them, often instantly on contact. Mark had no pretensions; he was willing to work with you just as long as you were willing to work and keep striving.

Many of these young people were drawn to the teachings of the ascended masters and to Mark Prophet and eagerly asked to join the staff of The Summit Lighthouse. Since many of them had taken a lot of drugs over the years and had no skill in the workplace, they could not easily be integrated into the older members of The Summit Lighthouse staff.

But Mark solved that problem! He pitched a tent on the back lawn, sent them over to the gatehouse for a shower, gave them a clean change of clothes and took them downtown for a haircut. After they had lived for a few days in the tent and drank gallons of carrot juice and fasted to detoxify, Mark invited them to work for him at the Four Winds. For many, this was the only job they had ever held in their life. Some had left home right after high school with a pack on their back and lived a life of traveling from one community to another—searching for that intangible "something."

Mark became a personal friend and a father figure to these young people—albeit a strict one. He provided the discipline that was missing from their lives and for which they had been longing. He taught them how to work responsibly and also gave them a sense of self-esteem, which many lacked.

I would like to relate an anecdote that one of the young men told me. He had newly come on staff and was feeling very lonely and burdened one night as he was washing pots and pans. Mark came up to him in the kitchen and said only, "Rruff! rruff! rruff, rruff!" (making a loud barking noise).

Of course you couldn't help laughing. And Mark said, "Now let that be a lesson to you, young man. Don't take yourself too seriously." He had his own individualized way of treating each situation with just the perfect remedy—whether it be humor, compassion, instruction or just plain friendship.

Some of Mark's original Four Winds staff are still on the staff of The Summit Lighthouse and Church Universal and Triumphant today. They are in their forties and some in their fifties; many are married and have families and now are able to fill responsible positions in the organization.

All succeeded because of the magnanimous heart of Mark Prophet. He really loved these young people and determined to help them in their search for the meaning of life.

These young people worked in various capacities in the Four Winds—from dishwasher to cook to sales force. They learned discipline and stability and, in the process, surrendered undesirable habit patterns and momentums.

They also experienced a one-on-one personal relationship with their guru, who was never too busy to take a minute to listen to them when he saw they were troubled. Some found a sense of family that had been lacking in their lives heretofore.

The Four Winds was definitely a success. Mark loved it! And so did all who came in contact with it. And incidentally, they and Mark became healthier as a result.

Gadgets

Mark was a person who loved gimmicks and gadgets. This love was apparent in his early life. He once said, "I was called a terrible child at eight. Do you know why? Because I took clocks apart. I took telephones apart. Any mechanical or electrical thing I could get my hands on, I took apart—whether it was in my home or someone else's. Well, it wouldn't have been so bad, but I did not always get them back together again, but I learned. By the time I was ten, I had ceased to do it. I learned!"

Mark had a pair of reading glasses that folded up several times until they were the size of a little miniature camera. He had a telephone in the car and loved to call in from wherever he was driving. All these little diversions offered a great reprieve for him from the intensity of his mission.

He liked to talk on a CB radio. He always had a radio in the car and he would talk to other CBers on the highway. And if someone was in distress, Mark would go and help them out. There were even CB clubs. It just happened to be his hobby.

There was a base unit at La Tourelle, and someone always had to man it because we could never know when Mark was going to call in. Some people use a few codes on the radio, such as 10-4 (I understand). But Mark used every code in the book. He would be talking and then drop into code: 10-99, 10-33, 10-27, etc. We had to keep a codebook handy to understand what Mark was saying.

Much of the time either the radio or our base unit would not work, or there was so much static that we couldn't understand each other. But Mark always kept trying.

Some people were judgmental of Mark Prophet and would say, "Why is a man who is so near his ascension and a messenger for the Great White Brotherhood being entertained by talking on a CB radio?"

Elizabeth Clare Prophet gave an answer to this question in one of her Summit University lectures. She said, "There are things that we do in this world that are human things. We are living in a human body. There are pleasures we need to experience. There are happinesses that we are entitled to. Happiness is a divine right. We're not martyrs. We're not gloom-and-doom people.

"And each one of us has our own preferences. Somebody may like gardening. Somebody else might want to play their guitar. Somebody else might want to do this or that, and yet they are not criticized for it. That is a part of the evolution and the integration of your being in God."

I am still certain that what many detractors classed as "Mark's idiosyncrasies" were his methods of temporarily relieving tension and stress so that he could be a better messenger, more closely attuned to God and the ascended masters. And then again, Mark loved life. He liked to have fun. And he enjoyed his CB radio.

Mark was very serious about security. Several of the homes in Colorado Springs had been burglarized recently and he decided to put in an alarm system as a warning if any problem should arise. And it was a beauty! There were strobe lights, bells, gongs, sirens, all sorts of alarms and flashing lights rigged up all over La Tourelle by one of our men who was interested in electronics. The interesting part of it was that the only "thieves" we ever caught were our own staff who forgot to turn off the alarm at the bottom of the stairs before they went up to their room.

I often worked late at night on *Climb the Highest Mountain.* I would obediently turn off the alarm before I went down to the kitchen for a snack. But it seemed inevitable that someone else, unbeknownst to me, would reactivate the system before I was ready to return to my office. Not only were the loud noise and flashing lights shattering to one's psyche, but all the men on the staff, including Mark, would instantly converge on the spot. There you were, staring at all these men in their pajamas, feeling foolish, and trying to apologize for disturbing their sleep. I can still hear Mark saying, "Oh, Mrs. Booth, not you again!"

The Laughing Bag

In addition to helping with the completion of *Climb the Highest Mountain,* in my spare time I was Mark's correspondence secretary. Now, that did not mean I ever wrote any letters for him—he had two secretaries for that function. I was in charge of all his *junk mail!*

We spent hours poring over catalogue and direct mail advertisements for belts, ties, wallets, boots, shirts, etc. By the time Mark ascended, I had a four-drawer filing cabinet completely full of junk mail.

When I would say, "Mark, don't you think we should clean this out?" He would say, "Oh no, someday I might need to buy something like that." And, of course, I would dutifully continue to file and file and file. Most of the offers were outdated, but we still continued to keep them—just in case they might be useful someday.

This can be a real blow to one's ego, I can tell you, because I was not doing a single, solitary thing that was of any value whatsoever.

It wasn't until after Mark ascended that I realized that he was keeping me with him so that I could get to know him, how he felt, how he worked, his manner of disciplines. I finally understood that he was giving me instruction so that I could later be working with the various teaching centers and study groups throughout the world. Disciplines usually took place in Mark's office and so I was privy to his methods of discipline also. But it took me a long time to realize the reason for my being Mark's "correspondence secretary."

Now it is time to tell about that crazy laughing bag that became the bane of my existence. Some of you may have listened to our tape recording "Miracle of Joy" and you remember the sound of that laughing bag. One day Mark walked very seriously onto the platform during a staff meeting and unleashed this stupid thing. He had probably bought it in a joke store—"Ha, ha, ha, hee, hee, hee." Of course everyone went into hysterics. It was fun. It was a way of relaxing and everyone was enjoying it.

To his poor "correspondence secretary," however, it was anything but a miracle of joy. Mark was forever putting it into different drawers in his desk. In the midst of a serious conversation, I would open a drawer and that horrible thing would go off with its incredibly loud, raucous laughter.

This went on for weeks. Mark would say, "Mrs. Booth, get a letter out of that drawer." Open the drawer—"Hee, hee, hee, hee" goes this laughing bag. And of course Mark would be laughing also at my shock.

It came to the place that I was in such a state of nerves that I was afraid to open any drawer, never knowing when that thing would start to screech at me. One day Mark said, "Mrs. Booth, I need a certain paper." I said, "Oh no, you don't! The laughing bag is in there." He said, "Mrs. Booth, I promise you on my honor, the laughing bag is not in there." I opened the drawer; nothing happened. But a moment later when I opened another drawer, "Hee, hee, hee, hee," goes the laughing bag, unexpectedly. I must have jumped a foot off my chair. Somehow my sense of humor did not quite measure up to Mark's.

I think this was another of the ways Mark could partially release himself temporarily from his tensions when he was holding the balance for the earth and the many assignments he had from the Brotherhood. But, believe me, it did nothing to relieve the tensions from his poor "correspondence secretary"—me.

Elemental Life Obeyed Mark

There came a time when Mark was traveling so often to Santa Barbara and other spots for lectures and seminars that transportation became a problem. He found it more efficient (and fun, too) to refit an old Greyhound bus for a mobile home that would carry the family and several staff members on his trips.

He took great pride in rebuilding this bus and painted it gold. We always referred to it thereafter as the "gold bus." He even joined a mobile home organization and subscribed to their magazine.

It was the style at that time, if you owned a large mobile home, to tow a motorcycle along behind for convenience on trips inside cities. It was much easier to ride a motorcycle in city traffic than to maneuver this large bus and to try to find a parking place. And anyway, Mark had always wanted an excuse to ride a motorcycle.

I have already related Mark's relationship with the elementals, those little beings of earth, air, fire and water. I told you in chapter 6 how he stopped a rainstorm from destroying our luggage on our trip to Europe. The elementals loved Mark and in turn responded to his love and served him.

He could turn the hail back up in the sky. He could stop the rain. He could reverse the course of a hurricane and send it back out to sea. He could turn a fire back into itself. He could cause the thunder to roll across the sky. I have personally witnessed many of these feats.

Mark's control over the elements, using the power of God's love, was phenomenal. The beings of the elements* are the force that holds back cataclysm and serious weather disturbances to the best of their ability. However, when the conglomerate of mankind's anger, hatred and other negative emotions becomes more than they can bear, they must unburden themselves in all sorts of unseasonable weather, fires, earthquakes, hurricanes, floods, etc.

The next anecdote I would like to relate concerns one little elemental that felt familiar enough with Mark that he could play a game with him. One sunny, summer afternoon at La Tourelle Mark decided to go for a motorcycle ride. All of a sudden Mark came dashing in the gate on his motorcycle screaming, "Hey, stop it, stop it!" This one little cloud was following him, raining right immediately over him, and there was no rain anywhere else in the sky.

It was the most amazing sight I have ever seen. Mark was absolutely soaked, and the rest of us were perfectly dry. He said, "This little guy wanted to play, and I just couldn't get him to stop." You could never guess what would happen next when you lived with Mark Prophet, who lived in two worlds at the same time.

One day Mark received a phone call from the ladies in the Wilmington, North Carolina study group that a hurricane was bearing down on their property. The news report was that it was to be a devastating hurricane that would wreak serious havoc in their area.

Mark went into action immediately and made powerful calls to God and the elemental beings. We heard on the news later that, rather than touching land, the hurricane turned completely around and went right back out to sea. The weather bureau said they had never seen anything like that in all their history of charting hurricanes.

Hurricanes don't just turn around and go back out to sea. But this one did! The love that Mark was able to send to the elementals, soothed them enough that they could again shoulder their burdens

One staff member related an incident at which I was not present. On a trip to Hawaii, the messengers and he drove to the top of Haleakala volcano on Maui. They were traveling far above the clouds, about 10,000 feet above sea level. On the way down, the road was engulfed by clouds and they couldn't see the road ahead of them. There was a danger that they might drive off the narrow road.

Mark put his hand out in front of him right above the dashboard and chanted a mantra to the elementals. And like the parting of the Red Sea, the clouds parted and the road became visible. The clouds remained on both sides of the road as they descended the mountain to safety through a perfectly clear corridor.

Christmas Tree Sales

At one time I read in Yogananda's book *Autobiography of a Yogi* that a person should not have any unresolved desires remaining before they passed from the screen of life.

I had always been interested in Christmas tree farms and Christmas tree lots. I thought it must be fun to sell Christmas trees and be among the fragrance of pine for a few days.

A chance was presented to me in an unexpected manner to satisfy this unfulfilled desire forevermore. A young man came on staff around Halloween one year and said that he knew we could make a lot of money for The Summit Lighthouse selling Christmas trees. Since many nonprofit organizations engaged in this type of moneymaking venture at Christmastime, Mark Prophet was interested.

Mark just looked right through me and said, "Mrs. Booth would like to sell Christmas trees." I answered, "No, no, no, no. I wanted to do that years ago, not now." Mark told the young man to go ahead and that Mrs. Booth would be in charge of the Christmas-tree-selling project.

When Mark said that this project would need financing, I said that I could take $1,000 out of our savings account, unbeknownst to my husband, and replace it from tree sales. And so, for a month before Christmas we sold Christmas trees.

After a week or so I suddenly realized that this young man was not selling well and things were starting to go wrong. It looked as though I could never recoup my investment at this rate—especially since I had never told my husband that I had taken the money out of our savings account.

Mark came to me one day and said, "What do you think about our Christmas tree project?" I replied, "Not good. I'm going to have to sell these trees myself. I must recover my $1,000 investment." Mark said, "Good, I was just waiting to hear you say that. You are the one to make this project successful."

And so, for the next two weeks before Christmas, we sold Christmas trees and Christmas trees and Christmas trees. We learned how to flock, a process that was just beginning to come into vogue. You took small particles of flocking material and glued them on the tree via a vacuum cleaner or similar machine.

Well, we did not just flock white trees as most of the lots in Colorado Springs did. We used all the colors of the rainbow. You should have seen our threefold-flame trees—bands of blue, yellow and pink. They were an absolute eye-catcher on our lot and brought people in to look—even if they eventually bought a traditional green tree.

I really did have fun selling my Christmas trees, although it became a bit difficult in the cold, snowy winter of Colorado Springs. Since I had lived in sunny California for a number of years, I did not even own a pair of boots or gloves. I had to borrow all the necessary clothing from other women on staff, even to the boots. I did not want to invest in winter wear because I could never use it in Santa Barbara.

We made a nice profit for The Summit Lighthouse from our venture. And yes, I was able to replace my $1,000 investment. To this day, this has remained a secret from my husband. I don't know why, but the convenient time to tell him never seemed to arrive.

Violet Flame Laundry

I was privileged to be working with the messengers during the final days of editing *Climb the Highest Mountain*. We were on the last phases, and those of us who were assigned to the book were not supposed to do anything except work on the book. We were not even supposed to attend decree sessions in the chapel. I think Mark felt the pressure of his coming ascension and was determined to publish the book quickly.

One day I realized, to my horror, that all my dresses were dirty. It was in the early 1970s and polyester was in vogue. All that was necessary was a quick dip in cold water and then to hang them out on the line to drip-dry.

Mark came into the laundry room and said, "Mrs. Booth, what are you doing down here? You are supposed to be working on the book." I answered, "Well, Mark, all my clothes are dirty." And then I became flippant, which I soon learned not to do with Mark Prophet. I said, "You know, this really is a waste of time. I don't see why the violet flame shouldn't take care of my laundry for me."

He looked at me very seriously with one of those expressions that seems to see right through you and said, "Mrs. Booth, you just get so close to God that you become one with the violet flame, and then God will let his violet flame do your laundry for you. Now, get back to work." And he turned and left the room.

I think most of the things I learned from Mark as my Guru came in just these short little sentences that yet required hours for one to meditate upon and internalize. One of his memorable sentences was: "The only difference between a rut and a grave is one of depth. And the human race is often in a rut and also often in a grave."

Simha!

One of my early recollections when I first came on staff at La Tourelle was the time when Mark had his first heart attack—not a fatal one.

He related to us that he was lying in bed and El Morya strode into the room and said, "Simha!" a word in Sanskrit that means lion. He said, "Mark, are you going to lie there and be sick, or are you going to get up and get well? If you are a lion, as you are supposed to be, beat your chest and roar like a lion."

You remember I said that during an earlier embodiment, he was known as the lion of St. Mark. We could hear his lion's roar echo throughout the house, and Mark was well in a couple of days.

That was one thing that worried me when I was in the hospital in 1988 with my own heart attack. I couldn't quite see myself roaring like a lion. I was afraid that I'd be sent up to the psychiatric ward. But it certainly worked for Mark.

The Retreat of the Resurrection Spiral

On April 14, 1971, by a fiat of Alpha and Omega, the Retreat of the Resurrection Spiral was established as the place prepared where devotees of the sacred fire might come and learn from the messengers the disciplines of hierarchy and prepare for their ascension.

They could come to La Tourelle, which henceforth was to be known as the Retreat of the Resurrection Spiral, and prepare to balance their karma through invocation to the sacred fire and service to humanity. This process is known in the East as karma yoga.

Prior to the dictation each of us was asked to bring a flower to the sanctuary, wearing it upon our person as a corsage or in the men's lapels. During the dictation Omega called our attention to the fact that all our flowers had wilted and died.

And then, at the close of the dictation, our flowers were fully restored as immortelles, appearing as dried flowers, yet having within them the flame of the resurrection. We noted that for months thereafter all our flowers that were used in the sanctuary became immortelles.

CHAPTER TWELVE

A Tale of Two Cities

MANY YEARS AGO, when the messengers were first married, Saint Germain prophesied that one day there would be a "tale of two cities." He said that Elizabeth would be dictating in one city and, at the same time, Mark would dictate in another city.

And so, on February 18, 1973, this event, which had long been prophesied, occurred. The final lecture and dictation of Mark Prophet's final embodiment were delivered at the altar of the Motherhouse in Santa Barbara. He gave a lecture entitled, "You Can Become One with God", and a dictation from the Ascended Master Saint Germain, "A Tale of Two Cities."

Simultaneously, Elizabeth was in Colorado Springs on that Sunday morning and delivered a dictation from Jesus, "The Marriage Feast at Cana."

There is another crisscrossing also. Through Mark (in the dictation of Saint Germain), the future work through Elizabeth was announced. And it was through Elizabeth in Colorado Springs that the completion of the Piscean Age through Mark was announced in the dictation of Jesus.

The Torch Is Passed

On January 1, 1973, a little less than two months before Mark ascended, Gautama Buddha gave his annual New Year's Eve address. Each year at this conference he would reveal the thoughtform for the coming year. The title for the dictation this year was "The Torch Is Passed!" I'd like to include a short quote from this dictation:

"The thoughtform is the hand of God holding a torch of hope, of faith and of charity to the world, to all mankind. It is simply a descending hand, firm and strong as praying hands. For these are the hands of God. The left hand of God is hidden from view, but the right hand of God penetrates the cloud. And man beholds in the hand of God a blazing torch which must be passed unto another.

"And so each of you must understand that in the forthcoming year it is a solemn responsibility for you, if you would do the will of Heaven, to pass the torch to another while still fulfilling its destiny for yourself."

You can see that this thoughtform was preparing us at inner levels for exactly what was about to happen—the passing of the torch from Mark to Elizabeth and ourselves, to the entire organization. Mark was passing that torch to another while still fulfilling its destiny for himself.

This is the dictation of Gautama that also contained the passing of the torch of illumination from the Regent Mother of the Flame, the Ascended Lady Master Clara Louise, to Elizabeth Clare Prophet. The passing of this torch included a dispensation for Summit University, for Montessori International, for the illumination of the world and for the teaching of all the world's children. There are several different levels of understanding in the dictation.

Torches must always be passed. One day you will pass a torch. The most important thing to remember about the passing of a torch is that the torch is a flame that burns. It is composed of many, many millions of little flames. And each one of these flames is a petal of light and sacred fire.

As you fashion your torch of life, you will want to be certain, as those who have gone before us were certain, that the torch will contain all that the one who follows you on the Path will need to make it all the way home in the victory of the ascension.

Mark signed Elizabeth's copy of *Climb the Highest Mountain* with the words, "May you win all the way!" It is not enough that we wish someone victory or winning. We want them to win all the way, every step of the way—not just today but to the hour of their ascension.

The torch must be there and burning. The torches of Gautama Buddha, Clara Louise and our own beloved Mark were there—just seven weeks before his ascension.

Lord Gautama made another comment in his dictation that sounded like Mark was putting on his Godhead and preparing to make his ascension.

He said, "Will you realize, then, that the dawn of purpose is to be perceived right before your gaze. For behold, the kingdom of heaven is with men. And the incoming of the Christ, although it appear as a thief in the night—one being taken and the other left (Matt. 24:40)—is still the miracle of the ages, extending itself to all ages."

"You Can Become One with God!"

May I quote from Mark's final sermon in Santa Barbara: "Ladies and gentlemen, it gives me great pleasure to be able to come here in Santa Barbara quite unexpectedly. I find that shortly I will be leaving California.

"I specifically want to invite you, all who are able, to attend the Easter conference, which will be held in Colorado Springs this year. I can promise you that there will be a large number of surprises that some of you may have anticipated and some of you may not. It promises to be a great conference, one that I hope you will not miss.

"But I know that if you knew all that was to take place, none of you would miss it—that is, I'm quite sure most of you would make every effort to get there. But on the other hand, I can't make premature announcements because I'm sort of caught in the jar of mystery. There are certain things that are restricted at this time and we are not announcing because we're getting ready to announce it. And we can't blow the whistle on ourselves.

"One of the essential elements of the path to the Godhead is captured in Jesus' famous statements: 'I go to prepare a place for you, that where I am, there you may be also.' (John 14:2–3)

'I ascend unto my Father, and your Father, and to my God, and to your God.' (John 20:17)

"From henceforth, the very being of God himself would be richer because it would have absorbed into itself all the magnificent Christ qualities that were externalized in the life of the man Jesus.

"Thus the universe is enriched by each soul who returns unto God crowned with the Christ Consciousness.* And through the law of rebirth, one is able to be reborn toward that more perfect day which will one day dawn when all sons and daughters of the Most High will at last express the perfection of their God—their individualized I AM Presence—in their life."

"You Can Become One with God!" Mark's last public sermon, contained all the keys to coming events short of the actual announcement itself.

On Monday morning, February 26, 1973, at Colorado Springs Mark made his transition. From inner levels his soul entered the fiery coil of the ascension and reunited with the divine Presence, the I AM THAT I AM.

Only days before, his parting words to his chelas were heard to resound in the rotunda of La Tourelle, "Death comes unexpectedly!" To Elizabeth he could only say, "Elizabeth, you'll miss me when I'm gone." Of course, she knew on the inner and had been prepared for this event for years, but at the actual moment it was a surprise to her, as it was to all of us.

And truer words had never been spoken. Not only would his wife, who was his twin flame, and his children miss him, but also a student body of thousands around the world would miss him more than they could ever tell. And for a planet and her people, the loss could not be calculated.

On February 18, eight days before his ascension, Mark L. Prophet preached his own ascension address—"You Can Become One with God!" That's as close as he would come to breathing a word of the secret.

A Safe Place in Montana

The night before his passing, Mark told Elizabeth that she should find a safe place in Montana where the community could be established and where headquarters could be relocated. He also gave her instructions concerning preparations for survival in case of cataclysm, nuclear war or economic unrest.

And so, after searching for several years, in 1981 we purchased the Royal Teton Ranch in Park County, Montana, on the border of Yellowstone National Park, in agreement with Mark's final instructions.

The Inner Retreat, Maitreya's Mystery School

CHAPTER THIRTEEN

"EXCEPT A CORN OF WHEAT FALL . . ."

ALTHOUGH MARK had warned us as much as he was allowed in veiled references to his imminent passing, we were completely unprepared when it really happened. One Saturday morning, as we were in a prayer service in the chapel, we saw an ambulance pull up to the front door of La Tourelle, and Mark was taken to the hospital.

He had suffered a massive stroke. Although he had had a number of small ones previously, he had been able to compensate for them spiritually and the effects had been barely perceptible to others. He suffered one in Santa Barbara during the New Year's Class, but on January 1, 1973, he had recovered sufficiently to take Gautama Buddha's dictation, "The Torch Is Passed!" The only lasting effect that we noticed was fatigue.

It was his time to be taken. He had told Elizabeth when they were married that he would pass in just a few years. The three years that he had expected had been extended to twelve. It was the time for his ascension, but physically that passing had to come through some physical means.

The easiest means was through a massive stroke, which could provide the painless and quick method of the soul exiting the physical body. Some of the greatest yogis have passed from the screen of life with a massive stroke because their bodies were supercharged with light.

Mark took his leave of us because his physical body was no longer adequate to the tremendous light of his being. You stay in the flesh as long as you can, and then you realize that you are immortal and that now you have an immortal light body.

Mother (as we called Elizabeth after Mark's ascension and after she had received the mantle of Mother of the Flame) was with him during his hours in the hospital. She and Mark were telepathing from the moment he had his stroke. He was kept alive with an artificial breathing machine from Saturday until Monday.

She asked him why he was going at this time and, of course, there were many, many reasons. But one of the answers he gave was taken from the Bible verse that begins in John 12:23, "The hour is come that the Son of man should be glorified." Glorified means filled with light, becoming radiant for the purpose of focusing the ultimate of the God consciousness and the Christ consciousness in the flesh form.

And then Jesus said to his disciples, "Verily, verily, I say unto you, except a corn of wheat fall into the ground and die, it abideth alone: but if it die, it bringeth forth much fruit." (John 12:24)

In that verse is contained the law of hierarchy: the law of laying down one's life in order that one's disciples may expand. There comes a time when, if the Teacher does not go on, the disciples of the Teacher cannot make further progress.

Mark often alluded to the principle of "the napkin" in his lectures. He would ask for a clean handkerchief, lay it flat on the table and pick it up at the center. You raise the center and the whole napkin will rise with it. The center that you pick up represents the ascending consciousness of the Teacher or Guru. That is what Jesus was talking about when he said, "And I, if I be lifted up from the earth, will draw all men unto me." (John 12:32)

Since Mark's ascension we all have more light in our bodies. He could only release this greater light to us by moving on and transcending the limitations of his physical body.

Through her inner sight, Mother was able to see Mark in all the glory of his immortal body while at the same time viewing all the evidence of human death on the physical level. He made his ascension only twenty minutes after he passed, after he was officially pronounced dead by the nurse who was taking his pulse.

Mother related that as she was standing by his side before it was time for him to go, although he had been totally paralyzed, he raised his right hand. He had not moved since Saturday, and this was Monday morning. He raised his right hand, took hers, squeezed it and blessed her. This was like the final blessing that Elijah had given to Elisha when passing his mantle to him.

We need to remember that the brain is not the mind. The brain is the instrument that the Christ Self uses to anchor the Mind of God in the planes of matter. This experience proved conclusively that the mind is independent of the brain.

Brain tests had been taken showing that there was no longer any functioning of the brain in control of the body— there was no activity in the brain. The control of the body that could allow Mark to raise his arm and hold Mother's hand was executed from the mastery of the messenger, not his physical brain. And so he was able to give Mother the final blessing to carry on the work as messenger for the Great White Brotherhood.

Mother described his passing in these words to a Summit University class: "Ten years passed, and it was almost as though I had forgotten that Mark had said he would be leaving shortly. In the meantime, we had had four children and ten thousand more other children who have become a part of our movement the world around.

"Suddenly one day in 1973, Mark passed on. He suffered a stroke in my presence, and within a matter of hours was in the octaves of light. I saw him after enduring the process we call death, or transition. I saw his soul leave his body, and I saw him received by Jesus Christ.

"A short time later I witnessed his ascension, the acceleration of his soul, his inner being, with the Spirit of God. I saw his soul rise into the Christ Self and then into the I AM Presence. And I actually saw at inner levels the ritual of his ascension.

"I saw the energies of the white light consuming the inner bodies, and in the case where one has not balanced 100 percent of his karma, as Mark had not, the physical body is not translated.

"And as the ascended masters instruct, that body is placed in the fires of cremation so that the atoms and cells, the light within, can be released into the sacred fire.

"He made his ascension February 26, 1973. And I saw him become a part, then, of the ascended masters, the sons and daughters of God who have gone before us.

"I think I experienced the greatest pain, as well as the greatest joy, that one can combine in the human life. I realized that this was the eternal liberation and the freedom of my beloved and yet realized that I would see him no more in the flesh."

CHAPTER FOURTEEN

LANELLO,
THE ASCENDED MASTER

Memorial Service

A few days after Mark Prophet's ascension on February 26, 1973, we conducted a memorial service at La Tourelle. Staff from the Motherhouse in Santa Barbara and Keepers of the Flame from all over the United States flew to Colorado Springs for this final tribute to our messenger.

It seemed as though almost the entire town of Colorado Springs (at least a goodly cross section of the town) arrived at our chapel. These were people from the filling station, the cleaners, the grocers, customers of the Four Winds—all who had known Mark when he walked among them and were eager to attend his memorial service when they heard he had passed.

And so there came to Mark's ascension service all these people from all walks of life who believed that he was just like them. They were there because Mark had stopped to talk to them here and there on the way.

Although we had often heard that "a prophet is not without honor, save in his own country" (Matt. 13:57), and although Mark had had detractors and criticizers from time to time, on this afternoon we could really see how many people had known and loved Mark Prophet. Those whose lives he had touched were happy to go out of their way to honor him.

Mother conducted the beautiful service herself. There was no grief displayed, only our great joy that our messenger had now ascended and would no longer be hampered by a physical body, which had become a great burden to him recently.

Mother with her children at Mark's memorial service

Mark had trained his twin flame well to carry on not only the mantle of the messenger but also the burden of the organization. We still had two messengers—one ascended and one unascended—as prophesied in the eleventh chapter of Revelation.

At the close of the ceremony, as I was standing beside Mother in the receiving line on the steps of La Tourelle, she suddenly pointed to a bluebird perched high on the turret of the roof, surveying the guests and singing happily. She said quietly to me, "Look, that is Mark."

We had known that ascended masters often projected their consciousness as a bird. And here was Lanello, greeting his friends again in the body of this little bluebird. We were overjoyed that this tangible manifestation of his presence could be allowed us as his gift.

Mark chose "Lanello" as the ascended name he wanted to be known by. Lancelot and Longfellow had been two of his previous embodiments, and so he chose to put these two names together as Lanello.

The Circle of the One

The staff felt momentarily bereft of our guru, to whom we had looked for guidance and direction. And so, for forty nights immediately after his ascension, Lanello met with us as an ascended master and offered us access to his Causal Body* of Light. The entire staff gathered at ten o'clock in the evening after our day's work was finished. We stood in a circle holding hands and praying. And then we dropped hands and gave the entire white section of decrees, the ascension decrees, one time through. From time to time Lanello would give us short private dictations during our nightly meetings, but his first public dictation was at the Easter Class 1973. Occasionally I still meet people who were present during those private staff sessions. They still remember the radiation that was released.

The Ascended Masters' Tributes to Lanello

Within a short time after the ascension of Lanello, each of the chohans of the seven rays,* the Maha Chohan* and the World Teachers* dictated a *Pearl of Wisdom** in tribute to Lanello.

El Morya, Mark's Guru and chohan of the first ray, said, "I say to you, one and all, those who grieve the loss of a dear friend and teacher and those of you who are able to rejoice in his glorious attainment, that because he has gone to the Father, he can add the momentum of his Causal Body* to your own that you might also do those greater works which were promised to the disciples of Jesus. (John 14:12)

"Each time a son or a daughter of God ascends, those who are ready to receive it are blessed by the presence of the Holy Spirit, the descent of the Paraclete.* And the communion cup of hierarchy* is shared once again with the children of God who yet dwell in the valley of becoming.

"The parting words of the avatar to those who gather round to receive the mantle of his victory must always be 'It is expedient for you that I go away: for if I go not away, the Comforter will not come unto you; but if I depart, I will send him unto you.' (John 16:7)

"I exhort you, O chelas of the will of God, to realize that the door to heaven stands wide open because your messenger and mine has opened it—not only for himself, but for you and all mankind.

"How can there be sadness in earth when there is

rejoicing in heaven? Never before in this embodiment have you had such an opportunity to pursue the flame, to feel its heat upon your brow and in your hand. For the cascading tides of life from the heart of the God Presence, from the heart of every ascended master now flow into your world over the pathway that he has trod before you.

"As Jesus spoke, so I say unto you, 'That which is born of the flesh is flesh; and that which is born of the Spirit is spirit.' (John 3:6) The best way that I can convey to you the meaning of the ascension is to liken it unto the birth of a tiny babe into its fleshy form, for the ascension is the birth into the Spirit.

'As man comes forth and bears the image of the earthy, so he returns to God to bear the image of the heavenly.' (1 Cor. 15:49)

"The ascension day of every man is the birthday of his immortal reunion with God, the day that commemorates the hour of victory when he becomes a pillar of fire in the temple of God, nevermore to go out (Rev. 3:12) into physical form to bear the burden of the sin of the world within his four lower bodies."*

El Morya told us that the newly Ascended Master Lanello can be seen "among them standing tall, clothed in robe of white and sash of brilliant sapphire blue."

Morya says that Lanello is repeating the mantra

> I AM free, I AM free
> I AM free forevermore!
> We are one, we are one,
> We are one forevermore!
> There is no death, no parting, no sorrow,
> But all-oneness, all-oneness
> And tomorrow and tomorrow
> and tomorrow.

Saint Germain also gave a tribute to Lanello. He said, "The pathway of salvation has been set before humanity by

The Ascended Master Saint Germain

countless avatars. The body temple is necessary to the evolution of the soul until the hour when the soul* merges with the Spirit* (the I AM Presence*) in the ritual of reunion that is called the ascension.

"Paul was asked, 'How are the dead raised up? And with

what body do they come?' His answer was, 'Thou fool, that which thou sowest is not quickened, except it die.' (1 Cor. 15:35-36)

"And then he proceeded to explain that there are 'celestial bodies and bodies terrestrial: but the glory of the celestial is one, and the glory of the terrestrial is another.' (1 Cor. 15:40)

"The four lower bodies [the memory or etheric body, the mental body, the emotional or astral body and the physical body] are the vehicles created by God for the soul's evolution. While in the physical octave, the anchoring point of consciousness is the physical body. But when transition comes—and come it must to all who are born of the flesh—then the soul's habitation is the etheric envelope and the etheric plane.

"That octave is a rarified replica of the physical octave. Its highest level shows forth the perfection of God and the pattern that is to be outpictured on earth. Here the retreats* of the Brotherhood are located and the fourteen etheric cities* that are found above the deserts and the oceans of the earth. Here life continues, and it is the memory of a sojourn in the etheric realm that enables mankind to believe in the continuity of existence beyond the grave.

"As an alchemist of the Spirit as well as of Matter, I see all of life as a process of transmutation, as that change from glory to glory of which Paul spoke. (2 Cor. 3:18)

"All things are indeed in a state of flux. Man rejoices as he anticipates changes in his life, the growth from one level of experience to another: from babyhood through childhood, the maturing years—years in which he masters the physical plane and the physical coordination of his body—and others in which he measures growth by soul development, by the conquest of knowledge, or by the expressions of the feelings of God as he learns to master his emotions and to express them as God would have him do.

"Some welcome death as a friend. They see it as an escape from their miseries, their failures, their wasted lives. Others fight death as an enemy—and well they should. For death is the last enemy that must be overcome (1Cor. 15:26) if man is to inherit immortal life as the logical transition of his consciousness out of the mortal socket and its experiments in the finite realm. Death is either the doorway to infinity or a point of reentry whereby man must eventually return to the finite to undo and redo and to finish that which he has left undone.

"Those who die in the consciousness of God and in obedience to his laws have nothing to fear, for to them death is but a transition to a higher glory."

Jesus also added his words upon Mark's passing. "You who loved him much have thought much upon his transition. I loved him too, as you loved him. And I know of the anguish that grips the heart when a loved one departs. If only momentarily, even the most advanced disciples must feel a pang of regret, a sense of loss when the teacher is called to higher service.

"How well I remember when the disciples of John the Baptist came and told me that Herod's daughter had demanded his head and that the tetrarch bowed to the will of that daughter of darkness. (Matt. 14:1-12) For a moment in eternity I, too, was seized with a sense of loss, even though I had been prepared for the hour—even though I knew that the work of the Lord's messenger had been accomplished and that his time had come.

"For this is hierarchy—that the master who attains the ultimate will give that ultimate to the one who is to succeed him in hierarchy and then, in a final act of selflessness, lay down his life for his disciples.

"The greatest desire of every teacher is that his disciple shall take up that mantle and exceed his own attainment, doing those greater works which I promised to those who would believe upon me as the incarnation of the Christ consciousness.

"Unless the pupils excel the achievement of the teacher, unless they strive to break the records of those who have run the race before them, there can be no transcending universe, no expansion of God's consciousness. This is law; and if it be broken, the spiral of infinity must be arrested.

"Thus, the good shepherd giveth his life for the sheep. (John 10:11) The shepherd teaches the sheep to assimilate his consciousness, his mastery, the momentum of his good works, so that by the leaven of his God-awareness, the whole lump of their consciousness might be leavened and raised to newness of life and salvation." (Matt. 13:33)

Lanello, the Ever-Present Guru

The disciples who beheld the ascension of Jesus into the cloud of his I AM Presence were met by two men who stood by them in white apparel and said, "Ye men of Galilee, why stand ye gazing up into heaven? This same Jesus, which is taken up from you into heaven, shall so come in like manner as ye have seen him go into heaven." (Acts 1:11)

And so, now we have Lanello, our Ever-Present Guru. We call him the Ever-Present Guru because he is always appearing and talking to his chelas. Because of his ascension, you individually have access to heaven when and if you want to ask for it.

In his book *Cosmic Consciousness,* which Lanello dictated to Elizabeth Clare Prophet soon after his ascension, he offers us the momentum of his attainment, of his self-mastery in the cycles of time and space. We can enter into the heart of Lanello and put on the garment of his self-awareness in God. We can put on the garment of the Lord.

Lanello said, "Having come so recently from the planes of matter,* being so aware of the stresses and strains attendant upon life, I am in a unique position to assist you along the homeward way."

Write a Letter to Lanello

How? How do you contact Lanello and accept his offer of assistance? You write a letter to him. Write it in your own handwriting. Do not type it, for it is your personal handwriting that bears your radiation. Pour out your love to him. Tell him of your burdens, your fears, your hopes and your plans. Tell him how grateful you are for his ascension and ask him to show you how to ascend also. Tell him that you accept his offer of assistance and ask him to walk with you every step of the way Home.

And then, when you have written your letter, burn it in a metal pan or in the fireplace. We have been told that as the smoke ascends, angels bear your request heavenward.

The Electronic Presence of an Ascended Master

There is yet another way that I can suggest for you to contact Lanello. Ask that the Electronic Presence* of Lanello or the master of your choice be superimposed over your form before you go to sleep at night. You will find that throughout the hours of rest, all of the momentums of light of that ascended being can be absorbed into your consciousness, your four lower bodies.

Before you go to sleep at night say, "Beloved Father, beloved Jesus the Christ, beloved Lanello (or name the master to whom you are calling), send me the Electronic Presence of yourself and let that duplicate of your image rest over me and through me and in me while my body sleeps."

You will find that you will have within you when you awaken the full pulsation of that mighty flame that is his full-gathered momentum of the victory of the ascension currents.

You may call to a different master each night—not only to Lanello—and find that you are given mighty assistance that otherwise might take many embodiments for you to develop through your own inner training. Each master has his own flame and has overcome life's trials in different ways. Thus, instead of having to master the various elements of life yourself by trial and error, you can have access to the master's momentum of attainment.

The Electronic Presence of an ascended master is a duplicate of his God Presence, and asking for his Presence to be placed over you at night is one of the greatest keys to your ascension. If you form this habit of calling for the master's Presence over your body as you sleep, you will soon find that you will awaken with ideas and insights that are invaluable. By using this dispensation diligently, you can cut years off the time necessary to become a candidate for the ascension. The masters can teach your souls more easily while the body is asleep and you are not distracted by the many tasks and vibrations of everyday life.

Lest you feel selfish about calling to El Morya or Lanello or Jesus, afraid to disturb them when they may have some important cosmic work to perform, you should know that since they are one with God, they are omnipresent. They can be present at all places at all times.

You may call for the Electronic Presence of Lanello to be placed over you without in any way detracting from his own service to the light. Remember, the Electronic Presence of a master is a duplicate of the master's I AM Presence. The moment you ascend, you can be anywhere and everywhere throughout cosmos at any given moment.

Lanello Will Walk Beside You

And now, since Lanello's ascension, he has gone one step further. He has offered us his Electronic Presence during the *daytime* also. He said that he would walk beside us as we go about our daily lives. So, if you will it so, you are now able to live twenty-four-hours a day with the Presence of an ascended master over you.

You can call for Lanello's Presence as you go to sleep at night; you can call for him to walk with you during the day. Now you can always walk the earth with an ascended master overshadowing you.

For those of you who knew Mark Prophet in physical embodiment, know that his love for you now is even greater than when he was hampered by a physical body, which was a great burden to him at times. He is completely free now as the Ascended Master Lanello, and he can be with any of you at any moment you call to him.

Mark liked to joke about his name, Mark Prophet, before his ascension. He once said, "As Jesus wrote, 'He that receiveth a prophet in the name of a prophet shall receive a prophet's reward.' (Matt. 10:41) My reward is the ascension. My reward is light."

Lanello has said, "I am as near as the breath that you breathe. And there is nowhere that you can go that I am not, for I have projected an Electronic Presence of myself to each one of you who will receive me.

"And so, we too shall walk hand in hand, and at any hour of the day or night when you reach out your hand for mine, I will clasp your own."

When things get rough, as they will occasionally, just say, "Beloved I AM Presence, beloved Lanello, help me!"—that is all it takes. That is all he is asking for—just a quick, "Lanello, please help me. Lanello, come."

He continues, "And if you will receive me as a prophet of your ascension, then you can have my Electronic Presence walking next to you, and I will wear my own blue cape. And they will say, 'Look at those twins walking down the street.' For you will look like me and I will look like you and who will say who is ascended and who is unascended? For did they not have a little moment of trouble discerning the difference between Jesus and his disciples?

"So they will not know who is who. And I dare say that when the negative forces move their chessmen on the board of life to attack your lifestream, they may very well fling those arrows of outrageous fortune at *me!* And then they will have the reward of attacking an ascended master! And how do you like that?"

God bless our Lanello! He really loves us!

The Retreats of the Brotherhood Opened

At the close of each of the masters' tributes to the newly ascended Lanello, they invited us to visit their retreats. This was a wonderful dispensation, because seldom have these retreats been open to unascended souls while they were still in embodiment. We were invited to come while our bodies sleep at night.

Perhaps it would help in your meditation if you knew where these retreats of the masters are located so that you can ask to be taken to them at night to study. The retreats of the ascended masters that are in the etheric octave now were once physical in past golden ages.

The Temple of Good Will, El Morya's retreat dedicated to the will of God, is located in the etheric realm in the foothills of the Himalayas above the city of Darjeeling, India. The Brothers of the Diamond Heart who serve at this retreat under El Morya assist humanity's endeavors by organizing, developing, directing and implementing the will of God as the foundation for all successful organized movements.

Lanto, the lord of the second ray, the ray of illumination, serves in the Royal Teton Retreat, located in the Grand Teton Mountain Range in Wyoming. This is the main retreat of the Great White Brotherhood on the North American continent. Perhaps this is the first one you might ask to be taken to as you study at night. The masters of this retreat hold beginning classes in cosmic law nightly.

Paul the Venetian is chohan of the third ray of divine love, the pink flame. He is the hierarch at the Château de Liberté in southern France. He sponsors ascended master culture for this age and works with all who desire to bring that culture forth on behalf of mankind.

Next, we come to the great disciplinarian, Serapis Bey, chohan of the fourth ray. Serapis maintains the focus of the Ascension Temple at Luxor in Egypt. This is the place where candidates for the ascension are taken, and it is considered the most difficult retreat to enter. And yet, as a result of Lanello's ascension, Serapis is also announcing that he has arranged classes at his retreat, which may be attended by all aspiring to mastery on the ray of purity.

Hilarion, the chohan of the fifth ray, the green ray of precipitation and truth, was embodied as the Apostle Paul. He maintains the Temple of Truth on the etheric plane in Greece near Crete. Hilarion works with atheists, agnostics, skeptics and others who have become disillusioned with life and with religion.

He said on the occasion of Lanello's ascension, "The dispensation of hierarchy to open the way for mankind to walk in the footsteps of one who recently gave his all to the nobility of Truth and who in honor performed a mighty service to the Brotherhood enables me to invite all who espouse the cause of Truth to come in their finer bodies* to attend temple training— classes in Truth here at the isle of Crete."

Now, lest you think that this dispensation of the opening of the retreats to mankind was only a short-term dispensation following Lanello's ascension, let me assure you that they are still open today and only awaiting your call. Please take advantage of this great offer and get acquainted with these masters personally.

The sixth ray of ministration, service and peace is presided over by the Ascended Lady Master Nada. Hers is a purple flame, the color of violets, flecked with metallic gold and ruby. Her retreat is over the Holy Land in Saudi Arabia.

Now we come to the master of the seventh ray, Saint Germain. He holds a very important position in hierarchy in this age. Not only is he the chohan of the seventh ray of freedom, mercy, transmutation and ritual, but he is also the hierarch of the Aquarian age. The pulsation of the violet flame can be felt from his retreat over the House of Rakoczy in Transylvania and also from the Cave of Symbols in the United States.

The Maha Chohan, (Sanskrit), or Great Lord of the chohans of the seven rays, also offers the hospitality of his retreat. He said that the doors will remain open as long as there are some among humanity who are willing to make both the trek and the sacrifice that are necessary to enter the strait gate (Matt. 7:13-14) of the Christ consciousness.

The retreat of the Maha Chohan is focused in the etheric plane over the island of Ceylon. Pink-flame angels who serve the Holy Comforter tend the focus of the comfort flame, a white flame tinged in pink with gold at its base and anchored in a crystal chalice, decorated with crystal doves.

And now, the newly Ascended Master Lanello has told us that his retreat is located in the etheric realm over the Rhine River in Germany. There you may meet him at night while your body sleeps.

El Morya closed his tribute to Lanello on his ascension by saying, "May I introduce to you the Ascended Master Lanello, to whom you may now call and whom you may address, knowing well that the friend whose hand you shook, whose smile greeted you once, will greet you again in the eternal embrace of Love's victory won."

Land of Lanello

We had our first major conference following Mark's ascension at Land of Lanello, a beautiful retreat setting in Colorado, on the Fourth of July, 1973. This gathering was held on a large piece of property owned by The Summit Lighthouse, an excellent location for a ten-day out-of-doors event. People came from all over to camp and enjoy our first informal conference. We worked for days building a tent city, a cafeteria and all the necessary amenities.

One thousand devotees arrived to attend the conference and to enjoy the recreational activities this site provided. We were overwhelmed by the crowd, because about 350 was our largest audience prior to this date.

That was during the Easter conference, just after Mark's ascension, where Lanello gave his first public dictation. We filled every room at La Tourelle with this large attendance—even the bedrooms upstairs.

Our electrician wired all the rooms so that everyone could hear the conference even though all could not be in the sanctuary at one time. Each room was given a number, and everyone rotated from room to room for each event. It was sort of like playing musical chairs. At least, by this method, everyone had a chance to be in the sanctuary occasionally.

So, here we were now at Land of Lanello with 1,000 attendees, and we didn't quite know what to do with them all. But, would you believe it, Lanello dictated and said that there were 10,000 people with whom he had a heart tie. He said that if we had put up enough posters and other publicity, they could all have attended Land of Lanello.

Mother told us that at the moment of his ascension, she noted that drops of light were flowing from his Causal Body* as he was ascending. She said it was almost as a shower of light, almost like an umbrella, going out throughout the planet. And she said that each one of these drops touched a soul. I suppose that those were the 10,000 whom Lanello wanted at his conference. Maybe you who are reading this book are one of Lanello's 10,000!

How To Ascend

On the nineteenth anniversary of Mark's ascension, in 1992, Lanello gave a dictation through Elizabeth Clare Prophet which includes, I believe, the most practical, down-to-earth instruction on the ascension that I have ever found anywhere. I should like to quote excerpts from it from one who had so recently ascended.

> I come to touch you and to have you touch not only the hem of my garment, but that and much more. My touch is a touch of eternal Life I would transfer to you on this occasion of my ascension victory and on all occasions to come when I shall speak to you.

You have spoken so often of ascending and of your ascension and of the process itself and of the goal of life, but do you really know how to ascend?

Do you imagine it shall be a leap from a diving board?

Do you imagine it shall be some lofty flight?

Shall it be an automatic process?

Who will be the helpers and how much will they be allowed to help you?

How much momentum of ascension's flame must be in your own sails? How much fire of holy purpose must be sealed with such white-hot heat/coolness of intensity in the chakras as to enable you to receive the transfer of flame whereby your identity is sealed and not denied?

You know well that should you enter that flame prematurely, it would cancel out life. Thus, not prematurely but maturely you will enter that flame—and not until you have dedicated your life and the life beyond, if necessary, to garnering the threads of light, garnering the skeins of ascension's flame, wrapping it around each thread in the garment of the Deathless Solar Body,* calling to the angels and working with them to mend the flaws, to mend the tears.

Yes, beloved, how do you ascend?

You ascend daily! It is like mounting a flight of steps. You know not the count, for the steps represent each step that must be taken in life. How to ascend is to arrive at the top step at the end of this embodiment.

You cannot leap the flights or the spirals and turns, beloved. And you do not know how many steps you must take, for each one of you is at a different place on this staircase.

Since you do not know the end or the beginning, you must keep on keeping on. You must take a step a day, a day being a cycle of an initiation that might endure for weeks or months. But if you do not take the appropriate measures each day—those that you know so well—in terms of maintaining your harmony, the fire of your dedication, your decrees intertwined with meditation upon God, even as you invoke and meditate, visualize and affirm the Word simultaneously—if you do not fulfill in a day's cycle the requirements of a certain step, it will be much more difficult to fulfill it later. For the next steps come upon you and then you are overloaded.

It is not that you are overloaded with menial work, beloved. You become overloaded when you skip cycles of initiation and then do not know where to turn. The army has marched on without you and you are looking for the staircase—indeed.

So, each rising and setting of the sun marks a cycle whereby you mount those stairsteps. There are many things in the duties of the day that cannot be postponed to the next, for when they are postponed and the momentum wanes, so often the cycle is lost and the project is not completed. And how difficult it is to get that project done when you have to crank it up again and start all over! So understand that this is life—life that is measured by the soul and the heart and the Holy Christ Self.

I bid you, then, secure the moments. Secure them as the mind uses them to enter compartments of eternity. For time is indeed an element of eternity, as eternity has compartments of measurement. This time has many dimensions, as does the space of eternity, yet there is a correlation to your life here below.

Thus I say, neglect not the hours. Fill them with

joy! Joy is the very first principle of the ascension. Take two individuals – one who fulfills his assignments without joy and one who fulfills them with joy. The one without joy, beloved, may lose his ascension for want of joy, and the one with joy may make it even though some elements are lacking.

"That your joy might be full" was the prayer of Jesus—and that you might know and have his joy remaining in you. This joy, beloved, can never be satisfied by human companionship alone but by a human companionship wherein those who are together see this as a vehicle for the divine companionship, for a divine joy that sprinkles laughter and merriment and play betwixt the hours of hard concentration. This joy that spans all octaves is pleasing to God.

Therefore I say, abandon a sense of martyrdom! Abandon a sense of self-condemnation! Abandon a sense of nonjoy! But take care that your joy puts God first.

Blessed hearts, joy flames go out when you are not in sync with your cycles on the staircase of life. There comes upon you a frantic sense of urgency within. You may connect it to outer responsibilities, burdens and debts, or to not having enough time to do everything you want to do.

Well, time will fall in place and so will space when you dedicate your day to meeting the requirements of the day's initiation on that step of your stairway of life. Then you will go to sleep at night in peace and have the peace of angels, knowing you are one step closer to the victory of your ascension or to the point of your adeptship where you may reincarnate again with a full 100 percent of your karma balanced.

Yes, beloved, your daily tasks and obligations have everything to do with your initiations on this staircase of life. Dispatch them well! Guard your time! Seal yourself to accomplish that which must be accomplished.

Only your Christ Self can solve those problems! Only Almighty God can solve them! And when you develop that attitude, you will dispatch those problems and dispense with them in a mighty short time and a mighty short space.

I ask you to devise a chart for each and every member of our staff and any Keepers of the Flame who would use it. And I mean this, beloved. Those of you who have imagination as well as a sense of organization should think about this. This chart is to be something you can use to check off tasks accomplished in the hours of the day. You can have it on your wall in your office.

And you and only you will know whether at the end of that day you can paste upon that chart a victory star—yes, beloved, a victory star: a gold star from having accomplished all those things that were on your list that you were capable of accomplishing, a victory star for not having let anyone deter you from that path and yet still having dealt with the needs of those who truly are deserving of your time and attention.

Blessed hearts, take control of your day! For it is a cycle of the earth, it is a cycle of your path of the ascension. This is how you make your ascension: I tell you, you score a victory each day! That means you must enter your day with a fierceness and determination.

Take the end of today to plan for tomorrow, to organize what you will do: when you will arise, who you will see and who you cannot see. Set goals and achieve them no matter what! For to break the patterns of letting things get by you, letting people interrupt you is no small task, but it is accomplished by the surefootedness of the compassionate ones. The compassionate ones, beloved, manage to achieve their victory and also accomplish their daily assignments.

A day's victory can become the victory of a lifetime. Count the days in the year and then the years in the decades of a life span and see how many victories you must achieve to finally step on the dais at the Ascension Temple at Luxor and feel the caressing love, the white fire of ascension's flame and hear the welcome of the seraphim who surround you and of all the adepts who themselves are candidates for the ascension.

Beloved ones, you will feel better about yourselves when *you* are in control of the hours of the day. Think of your victories as being moment by moment. Think of your failures as losing the moments and think of your lost moments as being added up into hours and days of nonachievement.

This is the point that I come to discuss this day: it is the hours that are lost because you have not filled them with the joy flame of Christ. And without the joy flame of Christ, your bodies will not be healthy, you will not have the strength that you need.

Joy is the key to healing! Joy is *movement!* Joy is *life!* Joy is self-attention to the needs of the four lower bodies, but not over-self-concern. Joy is the sense of committing oneself to God and letting God flush out the nonjoy by that descending cascade of the mighty river of Life.

O beloved ones, I have seen the days and the

hours of earth. I have reviewed my own embodiments. There is not a single saint in heaven nor an ascended master who does not look back on the record of his lifetimes with a great sense of loss and burden that in many of those lifetimes a certain percentage of the hours and the days was lost, lost to a pursuit of pleasure that was not required by the body or the soul but was merely an indulgence. I can tell you, we paid the price for those years and embodiments of indulgence, both you and I.

Now let us get on with life that is lived in the full zest of that joy of living, the *joie de vivre* that each one of you knows when you are in perfect attunement with your Holy Christ Self.

Something is the matter when joy flees from you! You must determine *what* is the matter. You must not suppress it. You must drag it out and look at it! You must see the phantom of the night, the ghost of the former self, and all of that psychology that you are working through.

I say, work *through* it! Do not simply tarry in working with it forever. Work through it and get beyond it!

Beloved hearts of Light, I speak to you with a profound love and a great practicality. I am practical and I see at inner levels how souls of Light upon earth do miss the opportunity for their ascension. Of course, when they do not have this path and teaching, they are not at an advantage but at a disadvantage. It makes us sad, indeed, to see those who have the Path and have the teaching and do not make it. For you understand, beloved, that it is possible for many more who have this teaching to make the ascension than actually do.

Well, what is the difference, beloved, between

those who do make it and those who do not?

I believe the difference is that those individuals who do not make it *do not take command of their own lives* but wait for someone else to command them and to take care of them. Taking command of your life and taking responsibility for your life means you take responsibility for the Path and the teaching and your daily service of decrees wherein you know you have accomplished what must be accomplished for that day's increment of your ascension.

And this is my point. You ascend a little every day imperceptibly. And if you do not take that little flame's point of acceleration in that day because of your failure to invoke the Light of God sufficiently, then you are not stepping up your cells and atoms gradually and you will not be ready for the full fire of the ascension pillar to pass through you.

What is the ascension flame but a million little flames?

What is a river of Life but a million drops of water?

Do you see, beloved? Each flame you accept and internalize each day (which is not a problem, for you scarcely notice the adjustment in your world), each little flame, then, prepares you to receive the great, great God Flame of your I AM Presence that is the ascension flame.

Beloved ones, observe your gaze, whether it be upon the mountains and upon your I AM Presence or looking about the world for someone, searching for this or that satisfaction or this or that attention.

Is there something that you yet want from this world?

Then tell yourself what it is. Ask yourself why

you want it and if it is worth the digression. Ask yourself if you can attain the satisfaction of that experience or that something that you want through the path of self-mastery and initiation. Or do you really need to go out and experience in some form that something that you find wanting in yourself?

Blessed hearts, more desires and longings for this world and the things of it can be satisfied by communion with God than you would ever dream of. The trouble is that people place their attention upon their desirings to such a great extent that they wind a coil of desire around the pole of being, around the spine. And each time it is wound, each time it is reconsidered, that coil of desire makes a stronger and stronger desire in them to do that thing that will take them from their God-centeredness.

But desire, beloved, is the most powerful force in the world. Desire will propel you to God and desire will take you to the very depths of the astral plane.

See, then, that you examine on this my ascension day the momentums of your desire.

Karmas themselves beget wrong desire. Therefore, be free! This is my message to you today. Be free! And the only true and lasting freedom you will ever have is the victory of your ascension in the Light. And short of that, beloved, you will know a certain element, and a powerful element, of that freedom *if you would take hold of your desires!*

Do not suppress them. But if you desire something that you know is not right, then go after that desire with your sword, with your Astreas,* with your Surrender Rosary, with your calls for the binding of your dweller-on-the-threshold.* Go after your wrong desires, beloved, and devour them by the sacred fire! For if you do not, they will only grow, even at the subconscious level, and soon they will devour *you.*

This is the single factor that takes people from the path of initiation. It is wrong desire. Pray to your Holy Christ Self that you might know what is wrong desire and the idleness of the mind and the misuse of time and space. Pray to know it. Pray to have that Christ Mind. Pray to the Presence of The Lord Our Righteousness.

Right desire can be known, beloved, in every circumstance. Therefore, seek ye first the kingdom of God and his righteousness, and all these things shall be added unto you. (Matt. 6:33)

You can consider yourselves in one sense of the word as mature sons and daughters of God with great knowledge of the Path and in another sense of the word as newly born babes yet in incubators, not able to live outside those incubators until you are strengthened.

So, there is a side of the nature that is fragile; there is a side of the nature that is strong. And again, beloved, it is relative, so that you know not when you are weak and you know not when you are strong.

Thus, the ascended masters do come and we do dote over you, but we do not indulge you. And we are fierce in challenging you when you allow yourselves to express the not-self. This cannot go unnoticed. This cannot go without discipline. This deserves the cosmic spanking because all of you know better and all of you are capable of doing better.

This is the significance of my coming today— to let you know that you can master yourself in the depths of those canyons of your own subconscious and unconscious. But you must be aware that that is what is happening in your life, for without awareness you may falter and fall.

Yes, beloved, it is wonderful to be with you. It is wonderful to be with you again and again. Make room for me in your office. Even a tiny picture of me will signal that I am welcome there.

My preference of a photograph is that which is before you. It is the one of myself on the *Sermons for a Sabbath Evening* album. This particular portrait I had taken in the full knowledge that I would be taking my leave of this world in the victory of the ascension. In this you will find my Electronic Presence* of Divine Love, for it was with the great desire to present to you a photo of my passionate love for your souls that I had this photograph taken. Thus I know that you will know me through that presence, through that look and through that heart.

I can do, oh, so much more for you, for I have that dispensation, being the co-founder with beloved El Morya of The Summit Lighthouse. Being now a co-guru with him and serving under him, I can do so much, beloved.

Don't forget to call to me, for Lanello is my name. Don't forget my little ones, all of the children in this community and beyond and those who are coming and those who must be on this path. There are so many that I hold in my arms. Don't forget to teach them to call to me and to tell them that Lanello is my name."

Mark L. Prophet

CHAPTER FIFTEEN

"Behold! I AM Everywhere in the Consciousness of God!"

MARK PROPHET opened the door to heaven for us all. That's how we know what we know about the Brotherhood and the path of the ascension. This is the meaning of the thread of contact.

He held it for us and never let go of it until he could place it in our hands and trust us to not let go. This is the meaning of hierarchy and the lineage of all who go before and after us. This thread is fragile and so is the grasp upon it.

"Behold! I AM everywhere in the consciousness of God!" That's the mantra of Lanello. And one day you can wake up and be there—not in the afterlife but right here and now, forever there and ever here. You can live in two worlds at once—in God's consciousness and yet fulfilling your physical responsibilities on earth.

This mantra is, was and ever shall be the communion of the saints that transcends all octaves and time and space, worlds without end: "Behold! I AM everywhere in the consciousness of God!"

Mark's hope for us was and is that our souls will rise in a burst of joy and creativity through the discovery that we can truly contact the Mind of God through the Christ Self and the sacred fire raised to the crown chakra. His hope for us is that the Mind of God in us will be the open door to eternity and to the fulfillment of the spirals of our Causal Bodies here on earth.

One of the key reasons that Mark took his ascension was to see to it that the children of the light upon earth might traverse the dark abyss of the astral plane and arrive at their proper position, either in the etheric plane or in the octaves of light.

He wanted to collect all of us together. And the only way he could do it was to be everywhere in the consciousness of God. And so he took his leave of us and ascended.

Mother gave us a message of hope after Mark's ascension. She said, "I know that through the sacred heart of Jesus and the immaculate heart of Mother Mary, Mark, as Lanello, has a direct tie to every soul of light on earth. I know that you can pull upon his mantle at any hour of the day or night and speak to him. Tell him of a need, personal or planetary, and he will answer that need to the fullest extent that the Great Law will allow.

"And I *know* that he is as fiercely dedicated to liberating each one of you here today and all who shall ever read these words as he was and is to liberating my soul unto the final victory of the ascension.

"For those of you who are beginning to understand the meaning of the fusion of heaven and earth through the Presence of Lanello, *know* that you have a Guru that you can hug. *Know* that you can hold on to that mantle and that you can tug. *Know* that you can talk to him, whether about the most mundane and simple things or about the most complex laws of the universe.

"He could explain the stars and he could point out all of the plots and ploys of the fallen ones designed to make us indulge our human consciousness and to detract us from the path of life."

Lanello is a man who always loved life and loved people. There is nothing that would have delighted him more than to have remained in embodiment for two- or five-hundred years going all over the planet, loving people and talking to them. He just loved to talk to people and never ceased to be interested in people of all sorts.

Mark used to travel across the country. And wherever he would go—a café, a drug store, a gas station—he would stop and talk to the working people. He loved the working people. Mark Prophet is the guru of the little people, the farmers, the laboring classes all over America—as well as everybody else's guru.

And so for him, to ascend was the ultimate sacrifice so that we could arrive at this point to serve in our mission. Mark worked hard and he worked long. He loved enough to master himself. Self-mastery is the key to adeptship. And Mark certainly demonstrated this.

And now as the Ascended Master Lanello, he still holds this love for us all. You may contact the magnanimous heart of Lanello, our Ever-Present Guru, through playing the melody "Greensleeves." The keynote of his identity is contained within the notes of this musical rendition.

Those of us who knew Mark have formed the habit of writing letters to Lanello, telling him of our wants and desires, our burdens, our hopes and wishes. We place these short notes either in our copy of *Climb the Highest Mountain* or in the Bible and leave them for Lanello to fill. And do you know, he answers almost all our ordinate desires—those that are in accordance with the will of God.

The answer is not always instantaneous, but it is fun to look back over our lists after a period of time and see how many have been answered. Perhaps you would like to join us in this exercise. It is not too late!

In Lanello we have our model for victory. He is our living Guru. Always remember that he is saying to you and to me, "You, too, can make it if you TRY! You can make it in this very life!"

Saint Germain has told us, "Death is either the doorway to infinity or a point of reentry whereby man must eventually return to the finite to undo and redo and to finish that which he has left undone."

For Mark Prophet, death and hell were swallowed up in Christ's victory. Truly, Mark lived and died and ascended for his principles and his loves, which were God's. He exchanged the body terrestrial for the body celestial (1Cor. 15:40) that we all might live. We have come to know one who walked among us, who knew God and who became one with his everlasting consciousness. He bids us do the same. He takes our hand. He shows us the way.

And yet, Mark traveled a long and hard road in this embodiment to find his way. It was not easy. He began a long, personal search, with many experiences and great disappointments in searching for God.

He found that the religions of the world, and even the alternative movements, were not always what he thought they should be. But he kept right on searching. And somewhere along the line, the Ascended Master El Morya made his appearance. We have all heard, "When the pupil is ready, the Teacher appears."

Mark relates some of his experiences and his philosophy:

"I was laughed at, called insane—even by people on the spiritual path. What kept me going in my search for God was the fact that I knew that God was real, and I had absolute faith that somehow or other he would show me the path that would enable me to do the work which I came to earth to do.

"For I believe that every life is a mission, and I think that each of you has a specific God-mission to perform in this world. I do not believe, however, that every mission is the same; each one is needed to complement the other. Therefore, we have to recognize that Western man has a job to do. And the time is short!

"There are hungry hearts out here in the world who are waiting for the message. You can do a lot as a divine mission-ary for God. But you must study until you know what you are talking about. A partial truth is as dangerous as error itself."

Mark often told us that he could not have made it on the Path without the overshadowing, care, compassion and wisdom of Mother Mary.

Many times he was bowed down not only by planetary karma but also by the weight of personal karma. He would emerge from all of this time and time again through the intercession of the Divine Mother. And now we have access to the intercession of Lanello, who is offering to help us over the rough places, as Mother Mary did for him.

In his book *Cosmic Consciousness* Lanello said, "Even now I am merging the attainment of my Christ consciousness with your own Holy Christ Self that my consciousness, merging with that of your own Higher Mind, might provide the bridge whereby this mortal might put on immortality, this corruptible might put on incorruption." (1Cor. 15:53)

We are left now, with the heart and message of America's twentieth-century Prophet and his mantle for any and all who will claim it.

So, as we pray to receive the mantle of Mark's magnanimous heart, let us again remember Longfellow's words:

> Lives of great men all remind us
> We can make our lives sublime,
> And, departing, leave behind us
> Footprints on the sands of time.

Mark, as the Ascended Master Lanello, now bids us follow in the footsteps he has so clearly left behind.

And he is saying to each of us, as he said to his twin flame, "May you win all the way!"

Mark and his twin flame, Elizabeth

Ours must be a message of infinite love,
and we must demonstrate that love
to the world.

—Mark L. Prophet

GLOSSARY

I would like to define certain terms that I have used over and over again in this tale. I have mentioned ascended masters, the Great White Brotherhood, hierarchy and retreats.

First, let's define **hierarchy**: Beyond this plane in the plane of Spirit, there is the foreverness of beings who identify as God, yet who retain individuality and awareness and identity because they have earned it. They have earned the right to be individuals because they have surrendered their will to the will of God and outpictured a certain momentum of light, of virtue, and so they are counted in hierarchy. Hierarchy, then, is the whole span of beings and their individualized consciousness that has been going on beyond our ability to comprehend. Beyond this cosmos, beyond this universe, beyond all that we know, God has been expanding life, and he will continue to expand life.

The **Great White Brotherhood** is an order of ascended beings serving in this system of worlds. It is the union of ascended masters of all who have graduated not only from this planet, but from other planets in this solar system and other systems in this galaxy. The Great White Brotherhood is comprised, first of all, of all who have earned their ascension by passing through time and space on this or on any of these several worlds. They have mastered time, mastered space, surrendered the three phases of the ego—the carnal mind, the will and the intellect—merged their consciousness with God's, transmuted their karma and returned to the Source.

Who, then, are the members of the Great White Brotherhood as we count them from this planet Earth? They are the saints and sages of all ages. They are from East and West. They are the great spiritual lights, the great artists, the unsung heroes—people from every walk of life. They don't have to have a particular religion, a particular creed, except love and obedience and sacrifice; they have come through all paths that lead back to the Source and to the One.

The word "white" refers not to race but to the white light of the Christ, the aura, that surrounds these saints and sages "robed in white" who have risen from every nation and every age to be counted among the immortals.

Hierarchy functions through **retreats**. There are retreats of the Great White Brotherhood on the etheric plane, some connected to the physical plane, all over the planet. To these retreats souls of mankind are invited. You journey there while your bodies sleep at night; you study, you receive the knowledge of the law. And by receiving this knowledge, when you come in contact with the teachings of the ascended masters, you have a memory, you have something that rings true within your heart. You know you have heard this somewhere before—it is not new to you. It is not new because you have been in the temples and retreats of the Brotherhood.

It will be some time before you actually remember your experiences in the retreats, but by and by you will have flashes and memories, and you will think it was a dream. But it is not a dream. It is an experience that you have in your soul, out of your body, in your etheric body.

The retreats of the Great White Brotherhood have been established on the planet almost concurrently with the birth of the planet. A retreat is more than a place where an ascended master lives and receives chelas. A retreat is a mandala and a forcefield that is used by the solar hierarchies to release increments of energy to a planet and a people—necessary light energy that needs to be stepped down by the ascended masters and by their chelas for the distribution of that energy among mankind.

And now, who are the **ascended masters?** You can become an ascended master! I can become an ascended master! This is the nature of free will, which the soul was given when she was created.

Ascended masters are individuals who have used the energy of free will, coupled with the law of their own inherent reality, the law of their oneness with God, to demonstrate mastery in time and space. An ascended master is one who has mastered the energies of himself, the energies that flow and course through the being of man, of woman. An ascended master is one who has mastered his environment, his world. And that mastery—reaching a certain level and bringing the soul into congruency with her own Christed being and her own God awareness—has propelled that one into the reunion with God that is called the ascension in the light.

Those who are the ascended masters have proven the victory over sin, disease, death and every conflict. They have balanced what in the East is called karma and in the West sin. They have balanced all energies that have ever been given into their use in all incarnations, and they have returned to the heart of the I AM THAT I AM.

The ascended masters have walked the earth as you and I yet walk this earth. They teach the law of reembodiment. They are important to us because they have proved the laws that we are in the process of proving. The ascended masters are the teachers who teach by example, not by words and platitudes. They are important because they reveal to us the next step of evolution. They point the way and they say: "I AM the way. This is the way, and the way ye know." They show that this way can be followed. They show that by proving the laws of God we can attain immortality and an immortal individuality, that all that we strive for and all that we are is not lost at the moment of death but is perpetuated by the action of that light that lighteth every man that cometh into the world.

When we come into the knowledge of the ascended masters, we come into an awareness of the Path. We find that the path back to the Source can be walked over seven rays of the Christ consciousness that emerge from the white light. I would like to talk to you about seven masters who have mastered identity by walking these paths.

I would like to define these paths and show you that there are archetypes of Christhood, that there are many paths, that you will find yourself on one of these paths by relating yourself to these masters. You will see that if you cannot totally meet the archetype of Jesus, who ascended on the sixth ray, perhaps you will find that your path is on the second ray or the seventh ray or any other of the rays.

These masters are called the **chohans of the rays**, which means lord of the rays. "Chohan" is the Sanskrit term for lord, and lord is equivalent to law; hence the chohan is the action of the law of the ray. It means that he defines that law. Through him that energy of the Christ and of God flows to mankind, to all who are evolving on that particular path.

The chohans are the closest ascended masters to us, to disciples in this age, to those who would be chelas of the real gurus. They are merged with Spirit, with the I AM Presence. They function in planes of perfection, but these planes are simultaneously one with matter where we are. And so the chohans are here with us. There is a congruency of Spirit and matter where we are, and we understand that time and space are but coordinates of infinity.

They retain in their service legions of angelic hosts and ascended brethren who carry out the plan of the Great White Brotherhood for the most complete expression of the **seven rays** that is possible among mankind of earth. Individuals are keyed to certain rays in order that they may perform a specific service to God and man. The ray of service to which an individual is attuned may vary from one embodiment to the next. But the reward for service is cumulative, and thus powerful momentums may be retained from one's past service on several or all of the rays. A balance of the seven is a requirement for the ascension and the mark of the golden-age man.

Statesmen, leaders and organizers are on the first ray under El Morya; teachers, philosophers and educators serve on the second ray under Lanto; artists, designers, beauticians and those of a creative nature serve on the third ray under Paul the Venetian; architects, planners and those dedicated to the purity and discipline of any undertaking serve with Serapis Bey on the fourth ray; doctors, scientists, healers, musicians, mathematicians and those consecrated to truth serve on the fifth ray with Hilarion; ministers, nurses and all who administer to mankind's needs assist Lady Master Nada on the sixth ray; diplomats, priests of the sacred fire, actors, writers and defenders of freedom serve with Saint Germain on the seventh ray.

If a student finds that he is lacking in any of the godly attributes, he may make calls to his God Presence, his own Holy Christ Self and the chohan of the ray that he desires to amplify in his world. Great strides of spiritual progress can thus be made in a comparatively short time.

And remember, now that Lanello is also an ascended master, you may call for his Electronic Presence over you as you go to sleep and also ask him to walk beside you during the day and hold your hand.

I shall attempt to define other terms that may be esoteric or unfamiliar. These have been included in the text and denoted by an asterisk:

Akashic records. The impressions of all that has ever transpired in the physical universe recorded in etheric substance and dimension known as *akasha* (Sanskrit). These records can be read by those with developed soul faculties.

Alchemy. The spiritual science of changing the base elements of human nature into the gold of the Christ. In the Middle Ages scientists used these laws and techniques to change base metals into gold. The Ascended Master Saint Germain has written a book explaining the sacred science of alchemy. (*See also* bibliography.)

Archangel. The highest rank in the order of angels. Each one of the seven rays has a presiding archangel who, with his divine complement, an archeia, embodies the God consciousness of the ray and directs the bands of angels serving in their command on that ray.

Ascended Master. One who, through Christ, has mastered time and space and gained mastery of the self in the four lower bodies and the four quadrants of matter; one who has balanced the **threefold flame;** transmuted at least 51 percent of his karma; fulfilled his divine plan; taken the initiations of the ritual of the ascension and accelerated by the sacred fire into the Presence of the I AM THAT I AM; one who inhabits the planes of Spirit, the kingdom of God, and may teach unascended souls in an etheric retreat on the inner planes.

Ascension. The ritual whereby the soul reunites with the Spirit of the Living God, the I AM Presence. The ascension is the culmination of the soul's God-victorious sojourn in time and space. This reunion with God, signifying the end of the rounds of karma and rebirth and the return to the Lord's glory, is the goal of life for the sons and daughters of God. The soul puts on her wedding garment and ascends through her Christ Self to the I AM Presence.

Ashram groups. Small study groups started by Mark L. Prophet under the direction of the Ascended Master El Morya; for prayer, meditation and world service; study lessons used in these groups are printed under the title *Ashram Notes*. (*See also* bibliography.)

Astral plane. A frequency of time and space beyond the physical, yet below the mental, corresponding with the emotional body of man and the collective unconscious of the race; the repository of mankind's thoughts and feelings, conscious and unconscious. Because the astral plane has been muddied by impure thought and feeling, the term "astral" is often used in a negative context to refer to that which is impure or psychic.

Astrea. Elohim of the Fourth Ray of Purity; works to cut souls free from the astral plane and the projections of the dark forces. (*See also* Elohim.)

Carnal mind. The human ego, the human will and the human intellect; self-awareness without the Christ; the animal nature of man.

Causal Body. Interpenetrating spheres of light surrounding each one's I AM Presence at spiritual levels. The color bands of the Causal Body contain the records of the virtuous acts we have performed to the glory of God and the blessing of man through our many incarnations on earth.

Chakras. (Sanskrit for 'wheel,' 'disc,' 'circle.') Term used to denote the centers of light anchored in the etheric body and governing the flow of energies to the four lower bodies of man. There are seven major chakras, five minor chakras corresponding to the five secret rays, and a total of 144 light centers in the body of man.

Chela. (Sanskrit word meaning 'slave' or 'servant.') A disciple of a spiritual leader or guru. A student of a more than ordinary self-discipline— devotion initiated by an ascended master, the Buddha or the World Teachers, serving the cause of the Great White Brotherhood. An adherent of the Christ in the process of attaining self-mastery.

Chohan. Tibetan for lord or master; a chief. Each of the seven rays has a chohan who focuses the Christ consciousness of the ray. The names of the chohans of the rays (each one an ascended master representing one of the seven rays to earth's evolutions) and the location of their retreats in the etheric plane are as follows: first ray, El Morya, Retreat of Good Will, Darjeeling, India; second ray, Lanto, Royal Teton Retreat, Jackson Hole, Wyoming; third ray, Paul the Venetian, Château de Liberté, Southern France and also the Washington Monument, Washington, D.C.; fourth ray, Serapis Bey, the Ascension Temple at Luxor, Egypt; fifth ray, Hilarion, Temple of Truth, Crete; sixth ray, Nada, Arabian Retreat, Saudi Arabia; seventh ray, Saint Germain, Cave of Symbols, Wyoming, and Cave of Light, India, and the Rakoczy Mansion in Transylvania.

Christ Consciousness. The consciousness or awareness of the self in and as the Christ; the attainment of a level of consciousness with that which was realized by Jesus the Christ; the attainment of the balanced action of power, wisdom and love—of Father, Son and Holy Spirit—and the purity of the Mother through the balanced threefold flame within the heart.

Christ Self. The Universal Christ individualized as the true identity of the soul; the Real Self of every man, woman and child; the Mediator between man and his God (the I AM Presence); each one's own personal teacher, guardian and friend; the voice of conscience.

Color rays. The light emanations of the Godhead. The seven rays of the white light which emerge through the prism of the Christ consciousness are (in order from one through seven): blue, yellow, pink, white, green, purple and gold with ruby flecks and violet.

Cosmos. The universe conceived as an orderly, harmonious system; all that exists in time and space, including spectra of light, forces of bodies, cycles of the elements, life, intelligence, memory, record and dimensions beyond physical perception.

Deathless Solar Body. The weaving of this body of light is begun in the heart of your God Presence and is spun out of the light of the sun of that Presence as man below consciously invokes the holy energies of God. These energies are focused in the threefold flame within the secret chamber of the heart, raised back through the crystal cord to his Christ Self, and then transmitted to the heart of the God Presence. Thus, from the purified energies of the heart, this garment is gradually woven in preparation for the ascension as the wedding garment of the Lord.

Decrees. A dynamic form of spoken prayer used by students of the ascended masters to direct God's light into individual and world conditions. The decree may be short or long and is usually marked by a formal preamble and a closing or acceptance. It is the authoritative Word of God spoken by man in the name of the I AM Presence and the living Christ to bring about constructive change on earth through the will of God. The birthright of the sons and daughters of God, "Command ye me." (Isa. 45:11) "Let there be light: and there was light" (Gen. 1:3)— the original fiat of the Creator. "Thou shalt decree a thing, and it shall be established unto thee: and the light shall shine upon thy ways." (Job 22:28) (*See also* Heart, Head and Hand Decrees.)

Dictations. Messages received through the messengers of the Great White Brotherhood from Cosmic Beings, ascended masters, archangels and angels and delivered through the agency of the Holy Spirit.

Dweller-on-the-threshold. A term sometimes used to designate the anti-self, the not-self, the antithesis of the Real Self; the nucleus of a vortex of energy that forms the electronic belt, shaped like a kettledrum and surrounding the four lower bodies from the waist down; contains the cause, effect, record and memory of human karma in its negative aspect.

Dhyani Buddhas. Celestial beings who, when summoned into action by spiritual devotees, bring the antidotes for overcoming the poisons that hinder spiritual progress.

Electronic belt. (*See* Dweller-on-the-threshold.)

Electronic Presence. A duplicate of an ascended master's God Presence, his I AM Presence. (*See also* chapter 14, page 159 of text.)

Elementals. Beings of earth, air, fire and water; nature spirits who are the servants of God and man in the planes of matter for the establishment and maintenance of the physical plane as the platform for the soul's evolution. Elementals who serve the fire element are called salamanders; those who serve the air element, sylphs; those who serve the water element, undines; those who serve the earth element, gnomes.

El Morya. The ascended master who is the teacher and sponsor of the messengers, Mark L. Prophet and Elizabeth Clare Prophet, and the founder of The Summit Lighthouse. The Chief of the Darjeeling Council of the Great White Brotherhood. Lord, or chohan, of the first ray of the will of God.

Elohim. The seven mighty Elohim and their divine counterparts are the builders of form. Elohim is the name of God used in the first verse of the Bible. "In the beginning God created the heaven and the earth." (Gen.1:1) The seven Elohim are "the seven spirits of God" named in Revelation (Rev. 4:5) and the "morning stars" which sang together in the beginning as the Lord revealed them to Job. (Job 38:7) In the order of hierarchy, the Elohim and Cosmic Beings carry the greatest concentration, the highest vibration of light that we can comprehend in our present state of evolution.

Etheric octave or plane. The highest plane in the dimension of matter; a plane which is as concrete and real (and even more so) as the physical plane but which is experienced through the senses of the soul in a dimension and a consciousness beyond physical awareness; the plane on which the *akashic* records of mankind's entire evolution register individually and collectively; the world of ascended masters and their retreats; etheric cities of light where souls of a higher order of evolution abide between embodiments; the plane of reality. The lower etheric plane, which overlays the astral/mental/physical belts, is contaminated by the mass consciousness and the lower society that man and his emotions have made of the earth plane.

False hierarchy. Beings serving darkness instead of light. (*See also* Hierarchy.)

Finer bodies. (*See* Four lower bodies.)

Fourteen etheric cities. Retreats of the ascended masters that at one time were cities in the physical but now have been raised into the etheric plane.

Four lower bodies. Four sheaths of consciousness of four distinct frequencies that surround the soul: the physical, emotional, mental and etheric, providing vehicles for the soul in her journey through time and space. The etheric body houses the blueprint of the soul's identity and contains the memory of all that has ever transpired in the soul and all impulses she has ever sent out. The mental body is the vessel of the cognitive faculties. When purified it can become the Mind of God. The desire or emotional body, called the astral body in Eastern literature, houses the higher and lower desires and records the emotions. The physical body is the one that enables the soul to progress in the material universe. The etheric sheath, highest in vibration, is the gateway to the three higher bodies: the Christ Self, the I AM Presence and the Causal Body.

God or Goddess. Terms used to denote ascended beings so named because of their complete and wholehearted dedication to the flame they have chosen to uphold and personify; a title and rank in hierarchy. These terms are not used in this text as a reference to the old pagan gods and goddesses.

Great White Brotherhood. A spiritual fraternity of ascended masters, archangels and other advanced spiritual beings; spiritual order of Western saints and Eastern adepts who have transcended the cycles of karma and rebirth and ascended into that higher reality. They work with earnest seekers of every race, religion and walk of life to assist humanity. The word "white" refers not to race but to the aura of white light, the halo that surrounds these immortals. The Brotherhood also includes certain unascended disciples of the ascended masters.

Guru. (Hindi and Sanskrit) A personal religious teacher and spiritual guide; one of high attainment; may be unascended or ascended.

Heart, Head and Hand Decrees. (*See also* Decrees.)

Violet Fire

Heart

Violet fire, thou love divine,
Blaze within this heart of mine!

Thou art mercy forever true,
Keep me always in tune with you.

Head

I AM light thou Christ in me,
Set my mind forever free;
Violet fire, forever shine
Deep within this mind of mine.

God who gives my daily bread,
With violet fire fill my head
Till thy radiance heavenlike
Makes my mind a mind of light.

Hand

I AM the hand of God in action,
Gaining victory every day;
My pure soul's great satisfaction
Is to walk the Middle Way.

Tube of Light

Beloved I AM Presence bright,
Round me seal your tube of light
From ascended master flame
Called forth now in God's own name.
Let it keep my temple free
From all discord sent to me.

I AM calling forth violet fire
To blaze and transmute all desire,
Keeping on in freedom's name
Till I AM one with the violet flame.

Forgiveness

I AM forgiveness acting here,
Casting out all doubt and fear,
Setting men forever free
With wings of cosmic victory.

I AM calling in full power
For forgiveness every hour;
To all life in every place
I flood forth forgiving grace.

Supply

I AM free from fear and doubt,
Casting want and misery out,
Knowing now all good supply
Ever comes from realms on high.

I AM the hand of God's own fortune
Flooding forth the treasures of light,
Now receiving full abundance
To supply each need of life.

Perfection

I AM life of God-direction.
Blaze thy light of truth in me.
Focus here all God's perfection,
From all discord set me free.

Make and keep me anchored ever
In the justice of thy plan—
I AM the presence of perfection
Living the life of God in man!

Transfiguration

I AM changing all my garments,
Old ones for the bright new day;
With the sun of understanding
I AM shining all the way.

I AM light within, without,
I AM light is all about.
Fill me, free me, glorify me!
Seal me, heal, purify me!
Until transfigured they describe me:
I AM shining like the Son,
I AM shining like the sun!

Resurrection

I AM the flame of resurrection
Blazing God's pure light through me.
Now I AM raising every atom,
From every shadow I AM free.

I AM the light of God's full presence,
I AM living ever free.
Now the flame of life eternal
Rises up to victory.

Ascension

I AM ascension light,
Victory flowing free,
All of good won at last
For all eternity.

I AM light, all weights are gone.
Into the air I raise;
To all I pour with full God power
My wondrous song of praise.

All hail! I AM the living Christ,
The ever-loving one.
Ascended now with full God power,
I AM a blazing sun!

Hierarchy. The universal chain of individualized God-free beings. The level of one's spiritual/physical attainment, measured by one's balanced self-awareness and demonstration of the use of God's law by his love in the Spirit/Matter cosmos, is the criterion establishing one's placement on the ladder of life called hierarchy.

Higher Self. The I AM Presence and Christ Self.

Holy Spirit. Third Person of the Trinity (Father, Son and Holy Spirit); the cloven tongues of fire, which descended on the disciples at Pentecost. In the Hindu Trinity of Brahma, Vishnu and Shiva, the Holy Spirit corresponds to Shiva. The representative of the Holy Spirit to earth's evolutions is the ascended master who occupies the office of Maha Chohan.

I AM Activity. Organization founded in the 1930s by Guy and Edna Ballard under the direction and sponsorship of the Ascended Master Saint Germain; brought to souls in the twentieth century the awareness of the I AM Presence, Saint Germain, the ascended masters and the violet flame.

I AM Presence. The I AM THAT I AM; the individualized Presence of God focused for each individual soul; the God-identity of the individual.

I AM THAT I AM. The name of God. (Ex. 3:13-15)

Karma. The law of cause and effect and retribution; also called the law of the circle, which decrees that whatever we do comes full circle to our doorstep for resolution. Paul said, "Whatsoever a man soweth, that shall he also reap. (Gal. 6:7) The law of karma necessitates the soul's reincarnation so that she can pay the debt for her misuses of God's light and energy. Thus, from lifetime to lifetime man determines his fate by his actions—including his thoughts, feelings, words and deeds. The transmutation of karma can be accelerated by invocations to the violet flame of the Holy Spirit.

Karmic Board. (*See* Lords of Karma.)

Keepers of the Flame Fraternity. Founded in 1961 by Saint Germain; an organization of ascended masters and their chelas who vow to keep the Flame of Life on earth and support the activities of the Great White Brotherhood and the dissemination of their teachings. Keepers of the Flame receive graded lessons in cosmic law dictated by the ascended masters to their messengers, Mark and Elizabeth Prophet.

Kuthumi. The ascended master who serves with Jesus in the office of World Teacher; responsible for setting forth the teachings in this two-thousand-year cycle of the Piscean age leading to individual self-mastery and the Christ consciousness; master psychologist; sponsor of youth; was embodied as Saint Francis of Assisi; also called K.H. who, together with El Morya, founded the Theosophical Society in 1875 to reacquaint mankind with the ancient wisdom that underlies all the world's religions.

Light. Spiritual light is the energy of God, the potential of the Christ. As the personification of Spirit, the term "Light" can be used synonymously with the terms "God" and "Christ." As the essence of Spirit it is synonymous with "sacred fire." It is the emanation of the Great Central Sun and the individualized I AM Presence—the source of all life.

Lords of Karma. The ascended beings who comprise the Karmic Board. Their names and the rays that they represent on the board are as follows: first ray, the Great Divine Director; second ray, the Goddess of Liberty; third ray, the Ascended Lady Master Nada; fourth ray, the Elohim Cyclopea; fifth ray, Pallas Athena, Goddess of Truth; sixth ray, Portia, the Goddess of Justice; seventh ray, Kuan Yin, Goddess of Mercy. The Lords of Karma dispense justice to this system of worlds, adjudicating karma, mercy and judgment on behalf of every lifestream. All souls must pass before the Karmic Board before and after each incarnation on earth, receiving their assignment and karmic allotment for each lifetime beforehand and the review of their performance at it conclusion. Through the Keeper of the Scrolls and the recording angels, the Lords of Karma have access to the complete records of every lifestream's incarnations on earth. They determine who shall embody, as well as when and where. They assign souls to families and communities, measuring out the weights of karma that must be balanced. The Karmic Board, acting in consonance with the individual I AM Presence and Christ Self, determines when the soul has earned the right to be free from the wheel of karma and the round of rebirth. The Lords of Karma meet at the Royal Teton Retreat twice yearly, at winter and summer solstice, to review petitions from unascended mankind and to grant dispensations for their assistance.

Maha Chohan. (Sanskrit) "Great Lord" of the seven rays; the representative of the Holy Spirit to a planet and it's evolutions; one who embodies the Trinity and the Mother flame of the seven rays and is qualified to be *Chohan* or *Lord* of each or all of the seven rays. Hence he is called the Maha Chohan, as he presides over the seven chohans of the rays.

Mark L. Prophet and Elizabeth Clare Prophet. Messengers of the ascended masters for this age; teachers, lecturers, writers; founders of The Summit Lighthouse with El Morya.

Matter or Mater. Latin for "mother"; the means whereby Spirit acquires, 'physically', fourfold dimension and form through the feminine, or negative, polarity of the Godhead; term used to describe the planes of being that conform to and comprise the universal chalice, or matrix, for the descent of the Light of God that is perceived as Mother; the Mother aspect of God.

Messenger. Messengers of the Great White Brotherhood are anointed by the hierarchy as their apostles to deliver the lost teachings of Jesus Christ through the dictations and prophecies of the ascended masters; one who is trained by an ascended master to receive by various methods the words, concepts, teachings and messages of the Great White Brotherhood; one who delivers the law, the prophecies and the dispensations of God for a people and an age. Mark L. Prophet and Elizabeth Clare Prophet, are messengers of God for this age. (Rev. 14:6; Matt. 10:6; 15:24)

Michael, Archangel. Archangel of the first ray, Prince of the Archangels, known as the Defender of the Faith and Champion of the Woman and Her Seed, who stands as the defender of the Christ consciousness in all children of God. He embodies God's consciousness of faith, protection, perfection and the will of God. From his retreat on the etheric plane above Banff, Alberta, Canada, he goes forth into all the world with his legions of blue-lightning angels to protect the children of light and preserve freedom on earth. Michael has fashioned a sword of blue flame from pure light substance to cut devotees free from astral entanglements. His keynote is the Navy hymn, "Eternal Father, Strong to Save." The keynote of his retreat is "The Soldiers' Chorus" from *Faust*. His feminine complement is named Faith.

Mother Mary. Mother of Jesus the Christ; twin flame of Archangel Raphael; also called the Blessed Virgin, the Blessed Mother and the Mother of God.

Paraclete. The Holy Spirit; the Comforter. (*See* Holy Spirit and Maha Chohan.)

Path of initiation. The strait gate and narrow way that leadeth unto life. (Matt. 7:13-14) The path whereby, through initiations, the disciple who pursues the Christ consciousness overcomes step by step the limitations of selfhood in time and space and attains reunion with Reality through the ritual of the ascension.

Pearls of Wisdom. Weekly letters of instruction dictated by the ascended masters to their messengers, Mark and Elizabeth Prophet, for students of the sacred mysteries throughout the world; published by The Summit Lighthouse continuously since 1958. They contain both fundamental and advanced teachings on cosmic law with a practical application of spiritual truths to personal and planetary problems.

Rays. Beams of light or other radiant energy; the light emanations of the Godhead which, when invoked in the name of God or in the name of the Christ, burst forth as a flame in the world of the individual. Rays may be projected by the God consciousness of ascended or unascended beings through the chakras and the third eye as a concentration of energy, taking on numerous God qualities such as love, truth, wisdom, healing, etc. (*See also* Color rays and seven rays.)

Real Self. The Christ Self; the I AM Presence; immortal Spirit that is the animating principle of all manifestation.

Retreats. Focuses of the Great White Brotherhood chiefly on the etheric plane where the ascended masters preside. Retreats serve many functions for the councils of the hierarchy ministering to the lifewaves of earth. Some retreats are open to unascended mankind whose souls may journey to these focuses in their etheric body between and during their incarnations on earth.

Sacred fire. God, light, life, energy, the I AM THAT I AM; the precipitation of the Holy Ghost for the baptism of souls, for purification, for alchemy and transmutation, and for the realization of the ascension, the sacred ritual of the return to God.

Saint Germain. The ascended master heirarch of the Aquarian age and chohan of the seventh ray of freedom; sponsor of the United States of America; teaches souls in the science and ritual of alchemy and transmutation through the violet flame by the power of the spoken Word, meditation and visualization.

Samadhi. A state of deep meditation leading to expanded awareness and higher consciousness.

Soul. Whether housed in a male or female body, the soul is the feminine complement of the masculine Spirit and is addressed by the pronouns *she* and *her*. God is a Spirit and the soul is the living potential of God. The soul can be lost; Spirit can never die. The rejoining of soul to Spirit is the alchemical marriage which makes her immortal through the ritual of the ascension.

Spirit. The masculine polarity of the Godhead; the coordinate of Matter; God as Father, who of necessity includes within the polarity of himself God as Mother and hence is known as the Father/Mother God; the plane of the I AM Presence of perfection; the dwelling place of the ascended masters in the kingdom of God. (When lowercased, as in "spirit," the term is synonymous with astral entities, or discarnates.)

Spoken Word. Disciples use the power of the Word in decrees, affirmations, prayers and mantras to draw the essence of the sacred fire from the I AM Presence, the Christ Self and Cosmic Beings to channel God's light into matrices of transmutation and transformation for constructive change in the planes of matter.

The Summit Lighthouse. An outer organization of the Great White Brotherhood founded by Mark L. Prophet in 1958 in Washington, D.C. under the direction of the Ascended Master El Morya, Chief of the Darjeeling Council, for the purpose of publishing and disseminating the teachings of the ascended masters.

Summit University. A modern-day mystery school for Aquarian age men and women of the twentieth century and beyond founded in 1971 under the direction of the messengers, Mark L. Prophet and Elizabeth Clare Prophet. Summit University currently holds two-week retreats each summer in July. Through the study of the teachings of the ascended masters given through their messengers, students pursue the disciplines on the path to the ascension that leads to the soul's ultimate reunion with the Spirit of the living God.

Threefold flame. The flame of the Christ that is the divine spark of life anchored in the secret chamber of the heart of the sons and daughters of God; the sacred trinity of power, wisdom and love that is the manifestation of the sacred fire; the soul's point of contact with her Source.

Transfiguration. One of the final major initiations on the path to the ascension. The transfiguration comes after the actual expansion of the light from within every cell and atom of the physical body as that light contacts the light of God in the universe. The light from within merges with the light from without, and you become a body of light on the instant. (Jesus' transfiguration is recorded in Matt. 17:1–9 and also

Mark 9:1–9.)

Tube of light. The white light that descends from the heart of the I AM Presence in answer to the call of the devotee as a shield of protection for his four lower bodies and his soul evolution.

Twin flame. The individual's masculine or feminine counterpart conceived out of the same white fire body, the fiery ovoid of the I AM Presence.

Undines. (*See* elementals.)

Vaivasvata Manu. The ascended master who is the manu of the fifth root race. (A manu is sponsor of a certain evolution or lifewave of souls who embody together and have a unique mission or divine plan to fulfill on earth.)

Violet flame. Seventh-ray aspect of the Holy Spirit. The sacred fire that transmutes the cause, effect, record and memory of sin, or negative karma. Also called the flame of transmutation, mercy, forgiveness and freedom.

World Teachers. Office in hierarchy held jointly by the ascended masters Jesus and Kuthumi. They are responsible for setting forth the teachings in the two-thousand-year cycle of the Aquarian age. They sponsor education at every level from preschool to college and university levels. They represent the universal and personal Christ to unascended mankind.

Zen. A sect of Mahayana Buddhism that teaches self-discipline, meditation and attainment of enlightenment by direct intuition by means of paradoxical and nonlogical statements.

BIBLIOGRAPHY

Titles from Summit University Press:

Saint Germain's Prophecy for the New Millenium by Elizabeth Clare Prophet with Patricia R. Spadaro and Murray L. Steinman

Lords of the Seven Rays *Mirror of Consciousness* by Mark L. Prophet and Elizabeth Clare Prophet.

Saint Germain On Alchemy *Formulas for Self-Transformation* recorded by Mark L. Prophet and Elizabeth Clare Prophet.

The Science of the Spoken Word by Mark L. Prophet and Elizabeth Clare Prophet.

The Answer You're Looking For Is Inside of You *A Commonsense Guide to Spiritual Growth* by Mark L. Prophet, compiled and edited by Elizabeth Clare Prophet.

The Human Aura *How to Activate and Energize Your Aura and Chakras* by Kuthumi and Djwal Kul.

The Great White Brotherhood *in the Culture, History and Religion of America* by Elizabeth Clare Prophet.

The Chela and the Path *Keys to Soul Mastery in the Aquarian Age* by Ascended Master El Morya dictated to the Messenger Elizabeth Clare Prophet.

Cosmic Consciousness *One Man's Search for God* by Mark L. Prophet as recorded by Elizabeth Clare Prophet.

Climb the Highest Mountain *The Path of the Higher Self* by Mark L. Prophet and Elizabeth Clare Prophet.

Forbidden Mysteries of Enoch *Fallen Angels and Origins of Evil* by Elizabeth Clare Prophet.

Dossier on the Ascension *The Story of the Soul's Acceleration into Higher Consciousness on the Path of Initiation* by Serapis Bey.

The Path to Your Ascension *Rediscovering Life's Ultimate Purpose* by Annice Booth.

The Lost Years of Jesus *Documentary evidence of Jesus' 17-year journey* by Elizabeth Clare Prophet.

The Lost Teachings of Jesus *Books 1–4* by Mark L. Prophet and Elizabeth Clare Prophet.

Quietly Comes the Buddha *Awakening Your Inner Buddha-Nature* by Elizabeth Clare Prophet.

Kabbalah *Key to Your Inner Power* by Elizabeth Clare Prophet with Patricia R. Spadaro and Murray L. Steinman.

Reincarnation *The Missing Link in Christianity* by Elizabeth Clare Prophet with Erin L Prophet

Ashram Notes by El Morya.

Creative Abundance *Keys to Spiritual and Material Prosperity* by Mark L. Prophet and Elizabeth Clare Prophet.

How to Work with Angels by Elizabeth Clare Prophet.

The Creative Power of Sound *Affirmations to Create, Heal and Transform* by Elizabeth Clare Prophet.

Access the Power of Your Higher Self by Elizabeth Clare Prophet.

Violet Flame to Heal Body, Mind & Soul by Elizabeth Clare Prophet.

Soul Mates and Twin Flames by Elizabeth Clare Prophet

Understanding Yourself by Mark L. Prophet and Elizabeth Clare Prophet

FOR INFORMATION
To place an order, request our free catalog
of books and tapes or for information
about seminars and conferences,
call 1-800-245-5445   (406-848-9500 outside the U.S.A.),
fax 1-800-221-8307   (406-848-9555 outside the U.S.A.),
or write to
Summit University Press, PO Box 5000,
Corwin Springs, MT 59030-5000 USA
E-mail us at: tslinfo@tsl.org
Visit our web site at www.tsl.org